# How to Make Friends

Enable You to Make Friends
Quickly and Easily

*(A Step-by-step Guide to Meeting People and Building Relationships)*

**Leo Marino**

Published By **Kate Sanders**

## Leo Marino

All Rights Reserved

*How to Make Friends: Enable You to Make Friends Quickly and Easily (A Step-by-step Guide to Meeting People and Building Relationships)*

**ISBN 978-1-7776028-5-7**

No part of this guidebook shall be reproduced in any form without permission in writing from the publisher except in the case of brief quotations embodied in critical articles or reviews.

Legal & Disclaimer

The information contained in this book is not designed to replace or take the place of any form of medicine or professional medical advice. The information in this book has been provided for educational & entertainment purposes only.

The information contained in this book has been compiled from sources deemed reliable, and it is accurate to the best of the Author's knowledge; however, the Author cannot guarantee its accuracy and validity and cannot be held liable for any errors or omissions. Changes are periodically made to this book. You must consult your doctor or get professional medical advice before using any of the suggested remedies, techniques, or information in this book.

Upon using the information contained in this book, you agree to hold harmless the Author from and against any damages, costs, and expenses, including any legal fees potentially resulting from the application of any of the information provided by this guide. This disclaimer applies to any damages or injury caused by the use and application, whether directly or indirectly, of any advice or information presented, whether for breach of contract, tort, negligence, personal injury, criminal intent, or under any other cause of action.

You agree to accept all risks of using the information presented inside this book. You need to consult a professional medical practitioner in order to ensure you are both able and healthy enough to participate in this program.

Table Of Contents

Chapter 1: Getting Involved On Campus .. 1

Chapter 2: Making Friends As A Commuter Student ..................................................... 16

Chapter 3: Making Friends In Your Classes ............................................................................ 27

Chapter 4: Making Online Friends .......... 43

Chapter 5: Making Friends As A Student With A Disability ..................................... 63

Chapter 6: Making Friends As A Veteran Student .................................................... 79

Chapter 7: Making Friends After Graduation ............................................. 91

Chapter 8: Understanding The College Social Scene ............................................ 97

Chapter 9: Places To Locate Friends In Campus ................................................ 105

Chapter 10: Utilizing Common Spaces . 115

Chapter 11: Balancing Academics And Social Life ............................................. 126

Chapter 12: Understanding Introversion ............................................................. 133

## Chapter 1: Getting Involved On Campus

Participating in university sports activities sports is one of the top notch techniques to fulfill humans in college. You might also moreover be a part of a membership or group that pursuits you, given that there are ones for pretty masses a few factor. Getting lively is a exceptional possibility to amplify your horizons, hone your abilities, and enhance your network.

Some Preferences for collaborating on campus:

Peruse the list of student sports activities sports. The Clubs and Organizations on Campus are all protected within the Student Activities Directory; this is to be had at most Institutions. The listing is often accessible online or at the scholar center.

Visit Club Expos. Club festivals are a fantastic possibility to find out new golf equipment and corporations and hook up with participants of those businesses. At the begin of every semester, membership gala's are regularly held by way of way of schools.

Talk to your unique college students. Find out, Grippe und Organizational your Classmates are a Part of, by using way of asking them. They may be capable to suggest a few corporations and organizations, you would love.

Don't be hesitant to offer something new a attempt. Don't be scared to try a few thing new, in case you're unsure about your hobbies. You may be stunned via how an lousy lot you need it.

Attend a few Meetings of the Clubs and Organizations you're interested by, after you've got diagnosed them, to see whether or not or now not they will be a suitable healthful. You do not need to determine to something except you're certain you want to enroll in, due to the truth the bulk of clubs and companies are great to new participants.

Below are some examples of the severa types of golf equipment and companies you could be part of on campus:

Clubs for college kids: Academic corporations are a super opportunity to satisfy other college college students who percentage your interests and examine greater approximately your important.

Clubs for the humanities and Culture: Arts and cultural agencies are a terrific opportunity to satisfy different students who share your hobbies and to specific your creativity.

Athletic and enterprise groups: Joining athletic and hobby golf equipment is a superb opportunity to fulfill exceptional students who share your interest in sports activities activities sports and health whilst moreover staying lively.

Community provider golf equipment: Joining a community company membership is a first-rate possibility to offer returned in your network and connect to fantastic university college students who percentage your enthusiasm for doing accurate.

Hobby Clubs: Joining a Hobby Club is a high-quality possibility to connect with specific college college students who have similar pursuits. There are agencies for nearly the entirety , which includes video video video games, anime, and outside sports activities sports like trekking and tenting.

Honor societies are educational companies that offer college college students with popularity for his or her educational accomplishments.

Associations for specialists: Networking with exclusive university college students and experts on your sector may be achieved thru expert agencies.

A brilliant way to fulfill new people, boom new talents, and beautify your network is to grow to be engaged on campus. Additionally, it's far a extraordinary possibility to bolster your résumé and be organized for lifestyles after college.

Below are more guidelines for making the maximum of your campus involvement:

Assume control positions. Consider assuming a manipulate function in your companies or companies, if you're interested in honing your management abilities. This can include taking over an officer role, taking element on a committee, or organizing a venture.

Participate in gatherings and activities. Throughout the twelve months, plenty of clubs and corporations behavior conferences and activities. These activities are a remarkable possibility to fulfill new humans, network with buddies and professionals, and function a outstanding time.

Give out it slow. A extraordinary approach to demonstrate your strength of will and make a difference is to volunteer a while to your club or institution. Additionally, it's far a great possibility to analyze greater approximately different individuals.

Getting working on campus is a exceptional way to beautify and increase your college experience. Additionally, it's miles a great chance to hone your skills, hook up with experts and exceptional university college students, and improve your community.

Additional mind for turning into lively on campus are furnished beneath:

Start your personal membership or agency with out hesitation. Consider developing your non-public membership or group, in case you can not discover anyone that appeals to you. It's a wonderful possibility to discover your interests and connect to other humans, who've similar ones.

Don't address too much. While it is vital to turn out to be engaged in college, you must no longer overextend yourself. Ensure which you have enough time to pay attention on your Schoolwork and one in all a type obligations.

A outstanding time! Participating in university sports activities ought to be pleasant. You're a good buy tons less inclined to persevere, in case you're not having amusing. Find companies and agencies which you are passionate about and like being part of.

Attending Social Events

It's a extraordinary possibility to meet new human beings and expand friendships to participate in social sports activities activities. On-campus social sports of many types, collectively with dorm events, fraternity and sorority gatherings, and scholar government-sponsored activities, get up regularly.

Preferences for going to social gatherings:

Don't overdress. Dress in a manner that makes you experience snug, because you want a good way to relax and enjoy your self.

Be right. Avoid attempting to be a person you are not, so you can in form in. When you act faux, others can be succesful to tell, and that they might not need to be round you as masses.

Be personable and high-quality. Introduce yourself, smile, and create eye-touch with people.

Be willing to interact with others. Don't restriction your social interactions to the ones you understand. Set up an Attempt to set up new friends and friends.

Take time to pay interest. People charge it, you deliver them a while and interest on the same time as moreover mastering them.

Don't drink too much. Making an exceptional impression is probably challenging whilst eating alcohol, for the cause that it could cloud your judgment.

A extraordinary time! Social gatherings are intended to be amusing. Therefore, unwind, have amusing, and socialize.

Some concrete hints for assembly human beings at social gatherings:

Find elements of settlement. Look for areas of similarity with the humans you stumble upon. Might be a few thing from having a same humorousness or mindset on lifestyles to sharing an hobby in a certain pastime or endeavor.

Pose inquiries. Ask them about their Interessen, Hobbies, and Personal Life, considering that human beings like discussing themselves.

Tell us a touch approximately yourself. Don't absolutely pose inquiries. Make fine to provide information approximately your self as properly. Diese will make it much less complex for the possibility character to get to apprehend you and determine, in case you click on.

Be empathetic and accommodating. Introduce your self, if you word a person who seems out of place or on my own. Introduce them to others or provide to tour them spherical.

A take a look at-up. Make positive to get in touch with the man or woman you meet at a celebration thereafter. You may also additionally additionally do this via contacting them thru social media or via inquiring for their cellphone amount.

Making friends through going to social gatherings is a excellent idea, however it's miles essential to keep in mind that it requires time and artwork. If you do no longer straight away set up loads of friends, try not to emerge as disheartened. You'll in the end meet your parents, if you absolutely keep placing yourself available and interacting with others.

Extra pointers for maximizing your social activities:

*Be there early. Diese will let you socialize and make new friends, earlier than the occasion turns into too packed.

*Don't be reluctant to socialize. Don't spend the entire night reputation although and speakme with the equal mother and father. Get out and socialize with new people.

*Take pauses. Do now not revel in obligated to spend the whole night time on the event. Take a pause to get some glowing air or to get a drink, if you're feeling overburdened.

*Be considerate. Respect the other attendees of the event, even in case you aren't having fun. Don't be obnoxious or disrespectful.

*Make a tremendous Impression. Be cautious to make a remarkable have an effect on on all people you find out attractive. Dieses involves being type, thoughtful, and engaged.

It may be lots of a laugh and a first rate way to fulfill new humans to wait social gatherings. Simply abide via those hints to maximize your enjoy.

Maintaining Friendships

It's essential to preserve the friendships you have already shaped, after you have completed so. Though effort and time are required, it's miles worthwhile. Your existence can be improved and made more profitable by the usage of friends. They let you in accomplishing your dreams and assist you get thru hard conditions.

The following advice can help you maintain your friendships:

Spend time together together along with your Buddies. Even if you're busy, it's also critical to locate time to your pals. Plan to fulfill frequently, regardless of the reality that it is most effective for coffee or a quick smartphone chat.

Be kind and perceptive. Through accurate instances and terrible, friends need to help every unique. When your friends are suffering, be there for them, and function staying power with them after they make mistakes.

Be right. To satisfy your pals, don't attempt to be someone you're not. When you act false, others can inform, and they may not want to be round you as plenty.

Be open-minded and truthful together along with your friends. Any healthful courting requires transparency and honesty. Tell your Pals the Truth about your feelings, critiques, and memories.

Be tolerant. Everyone errs sometimes. Try to forgive your Buddy, in the event that they offend you, after which flow into on. Keeping resentments ought to most effective make your friendship worse.

Basic recommendations for preserving your connections strong:

Prove your trouble on your Buddies. You can also do that via using doing smooth things like introducing your self in a textual content message or by way of giving them a token present.

Honor the accomplishments of your friends. When your friends achieve success, be thrilled for them. Inform them of your pride in them.

When your pals need you, be there for them. Be there for a Buddy who's struggling thru offering Support and Guidance.

Be confident in your potential to thank your pals. Inform your Pals of your appreciation for their friendship. Inform them of the tendencies you rate in them.

It takes time and paintings to hold friendships alive, however it's far worthwhile. Your life may be superior and made more worthwhile through friends. They can help you in mission your targets and assist you get via difficult conditions.

More thoughts on maintaining friendships:

The key is verbal exchange. It's crucial to stay in touch along with your buddies. You also can moreover perform this movement in man or woman, over the telephone, or on-line.

Be open to negotiating. There may be Moments, while you need to make compromises in conjunction with your pals, considering the fact that no people are exactly the same. Diseases require being ready to compromise along side your pals, however it does not suggest giving up on what is essential to you.

Don't expect a few issue about your buddies. Always preserve in thoughts that friendships are a gift. Spend a while displaying your Buddies how loads you charge and care about them.

Friendship renovation is critical to lifestyles. You may additionally additionally keep enduring and powerful friendships by way of the usage of the use of listening to these hints.

## Chapter 2: Making Friends As A Commuter Student

Although it is probably hard, making pals as a commuter scholar is clearly viable.

Here are some Pointers:

Participate on campus. Getting running on campus is one of the finest techniques for commuting university students to set up friends. You can also additionally be part of a club or group that pursuits you, because of the truth that there are ones for quite plenty anything. Getting energetic is a exquisite opportunity to increase your horizons, hone your talents, and beautify your network.

Assemble a look at organization. An fantastic technique to satisfy special college students to your guides and installation friends is thru becoming a member of a check business enterprise. Search online or ask your teachers or one of a kind university college students approximately Study Groups.

lunch on the campus. A exceptional technique to meet exclusive college college students and set up buddies is to have lunch on campus. Try to discover a eating place, wherein you may sit down and chat to one in all a type university college students, when you have a ruin among lectures.

Show as a bargain as campus sports activities sports. There are continually terrific sports taking place on campus, which incorporates athletic competitions, stay performance occasions, and talks. Making new Acquisitions in College is easy, at the same time as you're taking element in faculty sports.

Be inclined to have interaction with others. Don't restrict your social interactions to the ones you comprehend. Set up an Attempt to installation new friends and friends.

More recommendations for a commuting pupil to make friends:

Take initiative. Waiting for humans to return to you is vain. Make introductions and strike up discussions with others.

Be actual. Avoid trying to be someone you aren't, so that you can suit in. When you act faux, others may be in a function to tell, and that they'll now not want to be round you as a bargain.

Be type and perceptive. Through appropriate times and lousy, friends want to assist every one-of-a-kind. When your buddies are struggling, be there for them, and feature staying strength with them when they make errors.

Spend time along with your Buddies. Making time on your Pals is critical, but your disturbing schedule. Plan to fulfill frequently, even though it's handiest for coffee or a quick phone chat.

It takes effort and time to make buddies as a commuter student, however it is worthwhile. Your college revel in may be more suited and enriched through way of buddies. They can assist you in achieving your goals and assist you get thru tough conditions.

Other thoughts for installing friendships as a commuter scholar:

Never hesitate to are seeking out help. Never be embarrassed to are looking for help from your teachers, peers, or other pupil guide services, in case you are having hassle making friends.

Do not forget about which you aren't on my own. Many tremendous commuting college students are likewise having trouble making buddies. Make contact with other commuting university students and create a network of assist.

Be tolerant. Creating lasting friendships takes time. If you do not right now set up quite some pals, strive no longer to come to be disheartened. You'll in the long run meet your parents, if you surely hold placing yourself reachable and interacting with others.

Although it might be hard, making pals as a commuter pupil is in reality possible. You may additionally create enduring connections for you to enhance your college enjoy through using the advice in this passage.

Making Friends in Your Dorm

Benefits of dorm residing

Living in a dorm has numerous benefits, which includes:

Convenience: Because dorms are frequently determined on campuses, it is simple to get entry to education, the library, and other campus offerings.

Compatriotism: Making new pals and dwelling in a dorm are both extremely good advantages of doing so. You'll have lots of opportunities to mingle, for the cause that you may be dwelling close by other college college students.

Resident assistants (RAs), who're there to help college university students with their instructional and private dreams, are regularly visible in dorms. RAs additionally may be an first-rate aid for establishing buddies.

Dorms are often less expensive than off-campus-housing.

Advice on a way to get collectively along with your roommate(s)

You'll spend the bulk of some time to your dorm together with your roommate(s), so it's far important to take the time to get to recognize them and shape amazing relationships. Here are a few Pointers:

Be welcoming and outgoing. Tell your roommate(s) a hint bit about yourself and introduce yourself. Also be eager to research extra approximately them.

Establish limits. Early on, it's far critical to set up limits along aspect your roommate or roommates. This covers Details like noise degrees, bedtimes, and location visitors.

Be considerate. Even in case you don't land up being exquisite buddies, you must nevertheless apprehend your roommate(s) and their possessions.

Engage in open talk. Remember to be honest and obvious together together with your roommate(s), in case you are experiencing any problems.

How to make pals with other university college students in your dorm?

Here are a few suggestions for setting up pals with tremendous populace of your dorm:

Get active. Engaging in campus occasions is one of the greatest approaches to meet new humans and make pals. You may be part of a club or employer that pursuits you, because of the reality there are ones for just about some element.

Participate in sports activities held on campus. Throughout the year, hundreds of dormitories keep sports like potlucks, undertaking evenings, and film nights. Making pals at the ones sports is a first-rate manner to get to apprehend awesome dorm residents.

Be willing to engage with others. Don't restrict your self to the ones you recognize. Make an effort to introduce oneself to new human beings.

Be proper. Avoid looking to be someone you aren't, a very good way to fit in. When you act false, others may be in a position to inform, and that they may now not want to be spherical you as plenty.

Making a Community inside the Dorms

It takes time and work to create a dorm network, however it's miles profitable. A colourful dorm network may additionally provide you a constant, encouraging putting in which you may flourish. The following are some pointers for growing a dorm community:

Discover your friends. Try to get to recognize the opportunity college students that stay for your dorm. Simply greeting them whilst you see them or asking them for your room for a take a look at consultation or film night time will accomplish this.

Plan sports activities activities for the dorm. Putting on gatherings that deliver people together is one of the finest strategies to foster a revel in of network in a dorm. This may additionally additionally consist of potlucks, activity evenings, or movie nights, for example.

Be welcoming. Ensure that every resident for your dorm feels involved and welcome. Consider the histories and cultures of others and chorus from assuming some factor approximately them.

Be considerate. Even if you disagree with them or do not simply like them, show respect to all and sundry on your dorm.

Making pals in your dorm is a splendid manner to enhance and growth your university enjoy. You might also furthermore create enduring connections a excellent way to make your dorm seem like home by means of using manner of the use of the advice in this article.

Additional thoughts for setting up friends to your dorm are provided beneath:

Never be troubled to be who you're. When you act faux, others can tell, and they may not want to be round you as lots.

Be receptive to new topics. Meet new humans and try new matters. Who knows? You might also additionally click with them.

Be kind and perceptive. Everyone errs sometimes. When your friends want you, be there for them, and be forgiving when they lessen to rubble.

A remarkable time! It ought to be fun to visit university. Enjoy yourself and create some exceptional moments along with your new friends.

It takes time and paintings to establish a robust dorm community, however it is profitable.

## Chapter 3: Making Friends In Your Classes

Advantages of gaining knowledge of with friends

Studying along pals has a number of advantages, together with:

Academic overall performance is frequently extra even as scholars study alongside their buddies, consistent with studies. Dies ist due to the benefits of getting to know with buddies, which encompass

Increased records of the problem.

Find any locations of misconception and join them.

Learn from every different's numerous mastering philosophies and perspectives.

Studying alongside friends may boom your Motivation and preserve you extra chargeable for your paintings. You are lots a whole lot much less willing to take away reading or surrender when you have have a examine companions.

Reduced stress and anxiety: Studying alongside classmates may also aid in reducing anxiety and tension. This is due to the fact that studying with peers can also additionally make you revel in more equipped for exams and duties. Additionally, it might offer you get right of entry to to a community of sympathetic people.

Advice on the manner to make pals on your take a look at room.

Here are some recommendations for developing classmates:

Identify yourself. Introduce your self to the classmates you sit down next to in beauty at the start of the semester. Describe your self, which includes your name, area of start, and critical.

Pose inquiries. Ask questions and participate in discussions within the path of the elegance. It's a splendid approach to demonstrate your hobby inner the issue and hook up with unique college students who share the equal ardour.

Organize a have a look at employer. A look at employer is a exceptional opportunity to connect with classmates and accumulate help with the route content material. You may additionally furthermore look for check companies on-line or via contacting your instructor or different university college students.

Show up to beauty sports sports. Throughout the semester, many instructors installation sports activities for the elegance, which includes issue excursions, teachers, and potlucks. Making pals and learning your pals better also can every be finished by the use of attending those sports activities activities.

Establishing Study Groups

A amazing technique to fulfill classmates and acquire help with the path content fabric is to form a take a look at corporation. Here are a few tips for organizing a fruitful check group:

Look for classmates who get together with you. Look for buddies that percentage your getting to know alternatives, paintings ethics, and academic dreams at the identical time as figuring out who to embody on your take a look at group.

Decide on a everyday time and region for Meetings. Your Study Group want to set up ordinary Meeting Times and Venues. Diese will will can help you maintain organized and assure that everybody can attend.

Make a have a observe time desk. Make a have a have a observe time table outlining the subjects you'll be masking in advance than every meeting. Diese will help you in maintaining attention and maximizing some time collectively.

Be courteous and useful. Be type and considerate to all of the participants for your take a look at business enterprise. Inspire really every person to participate and to particular their thoughts.

Making buddies for your guides also can help you do better in beauty, be extra stimulated and responsible, and revel in much less compelled and disturbing. You also can make pals on your classrooms and create a welcoming learning environment thru the usage of the recommendation given above.

Additional thoughts for installing area pals for your school rooms are provided beneath:

Never hesitate to searching for assistance. Never be embarrassed to invite your college students or your lecturer for help, if you're having hassle know-how the situation.

Be real. Avoid looking for to be someone you aren't, with a view to wholesome in. When you act fake, others might be capable to inform, and they may not need to be round you as tons.

A superb time! Learning should be fun. Enjoy your self and create a few excellent moments with your new buddies.

Making Friends through Extracurricular Activities and Sports

Advantages of participation in extracurricular sports sports and Sports

Sports and extracurricular activities provide masses of advantages, including:

More educational improvement: Students who engage in sports sports activities and special extracurricular sports sports frequently outperform their pals academically, regular with research. Dieses ist due to the truth, taking part in sports sports and one-of-a-kind extracurricular activities can:

Improve it sluggish manipulate-capabilities.

Study hard attempt and intention-achieving strategies.

Establish a solid paintings ethic.

Improved physical and mental nicely being Maintaining your physical and highbrow fitness can be facilitated by means of taking element in extracurricular sports activities sports and sports sports. Dieses ist because of the truth, taking aspect in sports and different extracurricular sports activities can:

Exercise often.

Reduce anxiety and fear

Improve your temper and Self-self belief.

Possibilities for making friends Sports and extracurricular involvement are terrific tactics to satisfy new human beings and form friendships. Dieses ist , dass you may be participating with specific college students, who're passionate about the identical things you are.

Hints for gaining friends through extracurricular sports and Sports.

Here are some pointers for growing pals through extracurricular sports activities and sports sports:

Get energetic. The more possibilities you need to meet new humans and make buddies, the greater actively you are taking component to your extracurricular and wearing sports. Make an try to reveal up to all periods and activities and to take part in all of them.

Be personable and friendly. When meeting new humans, smile, set up eye touch, and introduce yourself. Be curious to discover greater approximately them and their passions.

Be empathetic and accommodating. Be supportive of your teammates and superb opposition. Offer Assistance and Support, within the event that they want it.

Be proper. Avoid trying to be a person you are not, a good manner to suit in. When you act faux, others might be capable to inform, and that they won't want to be around you as a excellent deal.

The exceptional sports activities as a way to have interaction in

Finding sports sports and extracurricular sports activities sports which you are interested by and that you like, is critical, due to the fact there are many one-of-a-kind sports activities sports activities and alternatives to be had. Here are some Preferences to help you choose out the proper sports:

Consider your Hobbies. What do you experience strongly approximately? What do you want to do if you have time off? You may additionally start searching out sports activities activities and extracurricular activities that in shape your interests, after you have got recognized them.

Talk in your friends and buddies. Find out what sports activities sports and extracurricular activities your buddies and classmates are taking component in. They may be capable to suggest some matters a amazing manner to do.

Visit Club Expos. At the begin of each semester, membership gala's are held at numerous institutions. Club festivals are a amazing opportunity to discover new sports activities sports and extracurricular sports similarly to connect to Individuals who take part in them.

Attempt new topics. Try new sports activities and extracurricular activities without hesitation. You can by no means ensure what you could like.

Making buddies through extracurricular sports activities activities and sports activities is a incredible method to boost your social existence, instructional achievement, and bodily and highbrow health. You may additionally pick the right sports activities activities and extracurricular sports activities for you and start making enduring friendships with the resource of the use of the recommendation given above.

Additional mind for meeting friends thru extracurricular activities and sports activities are furnished beneath:

Never hesitate to are searching for for help. Ask your coaches, teammates, or exceptional members for help, if you're having problem making pals.

Be tolerant. Creating lasting friendships takes time. If you do no longer right away establish loads of buddies, try no longer to turn out to be disheartened. Just preserve enticing inside the assets you need and putting your self accessible.

Making Friends via Volunteer Work

Advantages of Volunteerism

Volunteering has severa blessings, which incorporates:

Affecting alternate on your network. By volunteering, you enhance each the lives of other human beings and your Community. Can be a without a doubt pleasurable venture.

Acquiring know-how and new competencies. You may additionally additionally additionally growth new abilties and enjoy via manner of Volunteering, so one allow you to in each your personal and expert existence.

Making friends and interacting with new people. An top notch technique to satisfy new people and growth friends is through volunteer hobby. You will be taking element with Individuals that respect growing a distinction and share your values.

Advice on a way to discover volunteer opportunities

It is feasible to search for volunteer opportunities in plenty of unique approaches. Here are a few Pointers:

Search the net. Volunteer possibilities can be observed on various internet web sites. Volunteer opportunities can be positioned by means of using the use of area, reason, or skills degree.

Consult your spouse and kids and buddies. Ask any Volunteers , whether or not or no longer they'll be aware of any Possibilities, that might be of interest to you.

Speak with nearby organizations. Volunteers are essential to many community groups. To find out whether or not or now not there are any volunteer opportunities to be had, you may get in contact with nearby businesses.

Show up at volunteer fairs. Throughout the one year, a whole lot of community agencies and colleges have volunteer festivals. Volunteer gala's are a terrific opportunity to find out diverse volunteer options and connect to others who're engaged in them.

Forming relationships vIa Volunteerism

Here are some tips for setting up pals even as volunteering:

Be actual. Avoid trying to be someone you aren't, with a purpose to in form in. When you act false, others can be in a role to inform, and that they may now not need to be round you as thousands.

Be personable and satisfactory. When meeting new humans, smile, set up eye touch, and introduce yourself. Be curious to discover more about them and their passions.

Be empathetic and accommodating. Make yourself available to exceptional Volunteers. Offer Assistance and Support, within the event that they need it.

Be tolerant. Creating lasting friendships takes time. If you don't immediately installation quite some pals, attempt no longer to emerge as disheartened. Just hold networking and taking detail within the voluntary endeavors you discover amusing.

A high-quality opportunity to offer lower back on your community, meet new human beings, increase new abilities, and make pals is thru volunteer artwork. You also can furthermore choose out the proper volunteer opportunities for you and start developing enduring connections with the resource of the use of the recommendation provided above.

Here are some similarly thoughts at the manner to satisfy people thru Volunteering:

Look for volunteer possibilities in regions that hobby you. Diese will boom the risk that you may love your profession and meet others who percentage your ideals.

Participate within the nonprofit company. Do no longer certainly arrive, do your assignment and circulate. Attend social gatherings and specific sports to turn out to be greater active within the group.

Be inclined to have interaction with others. Don't restriction yourself to the ones you understand. Make an try to introduce oneself to new human beings.

A fantastic time! It want to be pleasurable to volunteer. Enjoy your self and create some notable moments collectively along with your new buddies.

Because it brings individuals together from all diverse backgrounds with the shared aim of changing the arena, volunteer paintings is a tremendous manner to fulfill new human beings. A strong foundation for friendship may be constructed even as you volunteer, because of the truth you're surrounded through way of people who percent your pastimes.

Consider volunteering, if you're searching for a way to fulfill human beings and alternate the vicinity. You can be stunned by means of way of ways smooth it is to installation new buddies and what kind of you wants the system.

## Chapter 4: Making Online Friends

Building ties with Individuals from all around the globe and assembly new human beings may be completed through making Internet Buddies. Making friends on-line can be completed in some of methods, together with via Social Media, on line Gaming, on-line Forums, and on line Communities.

Advantages of on line friendships

Making pals online has loads of advantages, collectively with:

Meeting new folks from other international locations online friendships are geographically unrestricted. You might also moreover connect to others who share your pursuits from anywhere inside the globe.

Locating oldsters with comparable pastimes. Finding others who proportion your pursuits can be loads of a laugh in online groups. Can be a exquisite approach to fulfill humans, with whom you can discuss your pursuits and from whom you may research.

establishing ties of assist. Online relationships may be clearly as sustaining as real-global-ones. Wenn you've got on-line buddies, you've got got Individuals, you may speak in self warranty to and who can useful resource you on the identical time as matters bypass tough.

Guidelines for final strong on-line

It's essential to exercising protection while developing net buddies. Here are some Pointers:

Be careful at the equal time as sharing records. Never provide non-public facts to any character you do not recognize properly, which includes your deal with or cellphone range.

When meeting people in man or woman, be cautious. If you do pick out to fulfill a person in individual, ensure to reap this in a public location and inform a chum or member of your family of your plans and anticipated move lower back time.

Any shady behavior need to be said. Report it to the internet website or the platform in which you noticed it, if you study a few aspect suspicious on line, collectively with a person seeking to catfish you or a person posting unlawful facts.

Locating on line companies, in which you could have interaction with one of a kind university students

You can also moreover have interaction with top notch university college students in a whole lot of on-line forums. Hier are some hints:

The Internet. The use of social media web sites like Facebook, Twitter, and Instagram to speak with extraordinary university students is substantially endorsed. You can be a part of communities and golf equipment which might be relevant in your pursuits, further to have a look at other college college students who intrigue you.

Gaming online. You may additionally moreover connect with one-of-a-kind college college students through online video video games, if you love playing video video video games. You can also be a part of guilds and clans and talk with unique game enthusiasts in pretty some online video games that have social elements constructed proper in.

Online communities and forums. There are numerous pupil-focused forums and corporations on-line. Your college, your important, or your pursuits may be protected through forums and agencies.

Be cautious to be energetic and participate in conversations, after you have got were given located a few on line forums, where you could interact with one of a kind university students. The best method to fulfill new people and increase connections is thru this.

Here are some extra recommendations for developing Internet Friends:

Be right. Avoid trying to be a person you aren't, an awesome way to healthy in. When you act fake, others may be succeful to tell, and they'll now not want to be round you as a good buy.

Be personable and exceptional. When meeting new human beings, smile, establish eye contact, and introduce yourself. Be curious to discover more approximately them and their passions.

Be empathetic and accommodating. Be present for the people you meet on-line. Offer Assistance and Support, if they want it.

Be tolerant. Creating lasting friendships takes time. If you do now not straight away installation lots of pals, try not to emerge as disheartened. Just maintain networking and taking component in the online agencies that you like.

Making buddies on line may be a superb manner to extend your social circle, installation connections, and pick up new talents. Making buddies is possible, in case you use the above recommendation.

Making Friends as an International Student

Although it is probably hard, making buddies as an global student is clearly possible. Hier are some advices:

Making buddies as an worldwide scholar might be tough.

Making pals is probably tough for remote places university college students for a number of motives:

A way of life wonder. It is probably difficult to modify to a present day manner of life and country. Making friends and adjusting to the cutting-edge way of life would possibly take the time.

Language Difficulty. It may be hard to have interaction with others and set up pals, if you do now not speak the nearby tongue of the kingdom you are transferring to properly.

absence of a guide community. You might not apprehend absolutely everyone whilst you to begin with relocate to a modern united states. Making pals and feeling supported can be tough due to this.

Hints for interacting with American and foreign students

Here are a few hints for setting up connections with each American and remote places university college college students:

Join corporations for distant places college college students. International scholar groups are not unusual in faculties and universities. These corporations are incredible locations to make buddies and network with different foreign places university students.

Enroll in guides along Americans. Try to join guides with American university college students, if the least bit feasible. Meeting American college university college students and studying approximately their culture may additionally each be executed via this.

Participate in after-college-sports. Participating in extracurricular sports activities is a fantastic opportunity to satisfy children from across the world and the usa. You also can volunteer for a purpose that topics to you or be part of groups and groups which can be applicable for your interests.

Be inclined to have interaction with others. Don't be shy approximately making small chats and introductions to new human beings. Be curious to find out approximately the backgrounds and cultures of others.

Constructing a Support Network

Building a help network is critical for foreign places university college students. Having a manual machine may also beneficial resource for your Socialization and Adjustment to your new lifestyles. Hier are some recommendations for growing a community of supporters:

Participate on your university or university's sports activities. You can also have access to a massive sort of materials and help offerings from your college or university. Use the ones Tools and Services to your benefit.

Make pals with college students from various countries. Other distant places college students may be in a position that will help you and relate to the troubles you are having.

Make friends with college college students from America. You may additionally make buddies with exclusive American college university college students and have a observe American lifestyle with the aid of American university college students.

Keep in contact collectively with your nearby u . S .'s family and friends. You may get emotional aid and motivation out of your friends and own family once more home.

Although it might be difficult, making pals as an worldwide scholar is without a doubt viable. You should make buddies with American and foreign places university students with the useful resource of the use of the recommendation given above, and you may create a assist community.

As an global scholar, you could use the following more advice to make pals:

Be real. Avoid attempting to be a person you are not, as a way to wholesome in. When you act fake, others might be capable to tell, and they will no longer want to be round you as a whole lot.

Be tolerant. Creating lasting friendships takes time. If you do not at once establish an entire lot of friends, strive not to turn out to be disheartened. Just preserve engaging in the matters you like and setting yourself on hand.

A super time! It need to be a laugh to go to college. Enjoy your self and create a few tremendous moments in conjunction with your new pals.

Making Friends as a Transfer Student

As a switch student, making pals is probably tough, however it's miles absolutely feasible. Hier are a few advices:

Making buddies as a switch scholar might be hard.

Making pals might be hard for transfer university university college students for some motives:

Having a weird feeling. Because they do now not realise all people and do not have the identical ancient past as the triumphing students, switch university students may also enjoy alienated at their new university.

Absence of a manual network. You may not understand everyone at the same time as you first of all be a part of at a trendy college. Making friends and feeling supported can be difficult because of this.

Acclimating to a modern placing. The transition to a brand new college may be quite hard. The new campus, the new publications, and the fashionable social environment must take some being used to.

Hints for interacting with modern-day and specific university college students similarly to alternate college college students.

Here are a few Preferences for interacting with present university college students and exclusive transfer college students:

Join groups for switch university students. Transferstudent organizations are normal in many colleges and universities. These organizations are first rate locations to make pals and community with first rate transfer university college college students.

Enroll in commands with gift students. Try to join guides with modern-day students, if in any respect viable. It's a exquisite chance to get to comprehend present university college students and find out the lifestyle of the school.

Participate in after-faculty-sports activities sports. Participating in extracurricular sports is an amazing possibility to get to recognize one-of-a-kind college students, each cutting-edge-day and switch. You may additionally volunteer for a reason that subjects to you or be a part of businesses and groups which may be applicable in your interests.

Be willing to engage with others. Don't be shy about making small chats and introductions to new people. Be curious to discover about the backgrounds and cultures of others.

Getting used to the contemporary college.

The following recommendation allow you to come to a decision your new university:

Learn about your campus. Spend a while becoming acquainted along side your new campus and coming across the numerous gadget and offerings at your disposal.

Speak collectively together with your instructors. Your teachers may be a valuable deliver of understanding and assistance. Attend your teachers' place of business hours and ensure to introduce your self.

Participate in Campus Life. An first-rate method to fulfill different university college students and experience part of your new college is to grow to be engaged within the community. You may additionally moreover take part in clubs and companies, supply decrease decrease again to the network, or visit athletic sports and other faculty-subsidized sports.

As a transfer pupil, making pals is probably difficult, but it is absolutely feasible. You may additionally moreover make friends with other switch students and normal college students, emerge as acclimated in your new school, and extra thru using the advice given above.

Additional advice for organising friends as a switch student is furnished below:

Be real. Avoid trying to be someone you aren't, as a way to inform in When you act faux, others is probably in a feature to tell, and they might not want to be spherical you as an entire lot.

Be tolerant. Creating lasting friendships takes time. If you do not right away set up loads of pals, attempt now not to end up disheartened. Just keep appealing inside the assets you want and setting yourself to be had.

A first rate time! It must be fun to go to college. Enjoy yourself and create a few splendid moments at the aspect of your new pals.

Making Friends as a Student of Color

A student of color can also additionally moreover locate it hard to make buddies, however it is truly feasible. Hier are some advices:

Making buddies as a student of color is probably hard.

A few barriers that scholars of colour can also have at the equal time as installing pals embody:

Racism and prejudice. Racism and Prejudice may be expert with the resource of university students of Color from their Classmates, instructors, or awesome college personnel. Being comfortable and making pals may be difficult as a result.

Not being represented. It is feasible for university children of shade to enjoy underrepresented in their lecture rooms or on campus. They have to enjoy by myself and lonely as a stop end result.

Microaggressions. Microaggressions may be directed towards university college students of color by way of manner of way of classmates, instructors, or distinct college employees. Racism in its subtlest manifestations, called microaggressions, can be ugly and alienating.

Advice for interacting with every white and black kids

Here are a few suggestions for interacting with every white college students and scholars of colour:

Join corporations for university children of color on campus. For university students of color, there are numerous pupil agencies in colleges and universities. These organizations are extremely good sources for connecting with one of a kind college students of color and developing a network of assist.

Attend guides with every white and colored scholars. Try to join courses that consist of every white and non-white students, if the least bit feasible. It's a top notch hazard to fulfill kids from all origins and discover one of a kind cultures.

Participate in after-university-activities. Participating in extracurricular activities is a high-quality possibility to satisfy different children, together with white university students and university students of color. You may volunteer for a cause that subjects to you or be part of organizations and groups which may be relevant in your pastimes.

Be inclined to have interaction with others. Don't be shy approximately making small chats and introductions to new human beings. Be curious to have a look at the backgrounds and cultures of others.

Establishing a network of cohesion

When you are a student of color, it's far important to create a help gadget. You can cope with the issues of racism and discrimination and revel in extra part of your campus network, if you have a supportive network. Hier are a few suggestions for developing a supportive community:

Join the multicultural middle at your institution or university. For students of coloration, multicultural facilities offer tools and help.

Establish relationships with unique university college students of color. The problems you're having can be higher understood and supported thru extraordinary university university college students of coloration.

Make relationships with pupils of colour. You also can set up connections with white university college students and find out about white way of lifestyles from them.

Keep in touch collectively with your nearby u . S . A .'s cherished ones and buddies. You may in all likelihood get emotional useful resource and motivation out of your friends and own family back domestic.

A student of shade might also additionally find out it tough to make pals, however it's miles truly possible. You can connect to university college students of coloration and white college college students via the use of the aforementioned recommendation, and you could create a supportive network.

Additional recommendation for college university college students of colour at the way to make friends is supplied under:

Be real. Avoid searching for to be a person you aren't, on the way to healthy in. When you act faux, others can be in a position to tell, and that they may no longer need to be around you as lots.

Be tolerant. Creating lasting friendships takes time. If you do no longer proper now set up some of buddies, attempt not to come to be disheartened. Just hold attractive in the belongings you want and setting your self handy.

A exquisite time! It want to be amusing to go to college. Enjoy yourself and create a few outstanding moments together along with your new friends.

# Chapter 5: Making Friends As A Student With A Disability

Even even though it is probably tough, it's far definitely viable for a pupil with a handicap to make pals. Hier are a few advices:

The difficulties a disabled scholar has in organising pals

Making friends might be difficult for Kids with Impairments for a number of reasons:

Stigma and prejudice. Students with disabilities may also stumble upon prejudice and stigma from their classmates, instructors, or one of a kind college employees. Being comfortable and making friends may be difficult as a quit cease end result.

Not being available. Accessibility problems can also exist for university kids with impairments on their campus or in their lecture rooms. Due to this, it can be difficult as a way to interact with amazing college students and take part in activities.

Isolation. Students with Impairments want to have a sense of social isolation. Dies will be due to the problems they encounter or others' lack of empathy.

Advice for interacting with Kids who are capable-bodied and university students with Impairments

Here are a few guidelines for making pals with every Kids with Disabilities and Students Disabilities:

Become a member of a student organization for disabled students. Student agencies for disabled university university college students are not unusual in faculties and universities. These organizations are first-rate assets for connecting with unique university students who have impairments and developing a supportive community.

Attend lessons with each succesful-bodied and disabled college students. Try to enroll in courses that consist of each succesful-bodied and disabled university college students, if the least bit possible. It's a brilliant risk to fulfill children from all origins and find out excellent cultures.

Participate in after-college-sports activities. Participating in extracurricular sports is a tremendous possibility to meet exclusive university college students, every in a position-bodied and university students with disabilities. You may moreover furthermore volunteer for a motive that topics to you or be a part of businesses and groups which can be applicable to your interests.

Be willing to engage with others. Don't be shy approximately making small chats and introductions to new humans. Be curious to find out about the backgrounds and cultures of others.

Defending your desires and pursuits

Being a pupil with a handicap way that you ought to speak out to your goals. Dieses includes speaking your desires to your instructors and awesome university students and searching out help while you do. Following are some Pointers for speakme out for your self:

Speak along facet your teachers. Inform your instructors approximately your handicap and the changes you need to attain success in their lectures. Make excellent to provide them with any assisting documents from your administrative center for disability help offerings.

Talk for your exceptional college students. Inform your Classmates about your Condition and the strategies they will help you. Be inclined to talk about your requirements and offer answers to their inquiries.

Participate in the pupil authorities. An fantastic method to speak out for the desires of disabled college students in your campus is thru pupil government.

Join an business commercial enterprise organisation that promotes accessibility. There are severa groups that propose for the rights of Individuals with Disabilities. A remarkable approach to network with special disabled humans and to fight in your rights is to sign up for a incapacity advocacy employer.

Even even though it might be hard, it is genuinely feasible for a scholar with a handicap to make buddies. By using the above advice, you may community with distinct disabled and succesful-bodied university college students, communicate up for your goals, and create a robust network of manual.

Here are a few extra hints for organising pals as a disabled scholar:

Be right. Avoid trying to be a person you are not, so as to in shape in. When you act fake, others can be in a position to tell, and they may no longer need to be round you as lots.

Be tolerant. Creating lasting friendships takes time. If you don't proper now installation masses of pals, strive now not to become disheartened. Just preserve attractive within the subjects you need and placing yourself available.

A extremely good time! It need to be a laugh to visit university. Enjoy yourself and create a few fantastic moments together with your new pals.

Making Friends as a First-Generation College Student

A first-technology college scholar also can locate it difficult to make friends, but it is truely viable.

The troubles a number one-generation university student has in establishing friends

Making buddies is probably tough for first-generation university college students for a few motives:

Feeling uncomfortable. First-generation university university students should feel uncomfortable at their college, considering they do not have the identical stories or cultural records as their Classmates.

Lack of assist. It's feasible that first-era college college students might not get lots assist from their loved ones and pals returned home. Making pals and adjusting to college is probably hard as a give up end result.

Financial problems. Financial problems may also make it tough for first-technology-college-university college college students to interact in social sports and set up pals with precise university students.

How to have interaction with present day and special first-generation university college students

Here are some hints for interacting with modern-day college students and distinct first-era college students:

Join groups for college college students who are first-generation. First-era pupil corporations are commonplace at schools and universities. These groups are splendid resources for connecting with unique first-technology university college students and growing a supportive community.

Enroll in training with existing college students. Try to enroll in guides with gift college students, if the least bit possible. It's a wonderful danger to get to understand modern university college students and find out the manner of existence of the faculty.

Participate in after-college-sports activities. The fantastic approach to meet one-of-a-kind university students, both first-technology college college students and current university students, is to end up engaged in extracurricular sports activities. You can also moreover volunteer for a reason that topics to you or be a part of agencies and corporations which are applicable to your hobbies.

Be inclined to engage with others. Don't be shy approximately making small chats and introductions to new people. Be curious to discover approximately the backgrounds and cultures of others.

Getting approximately in College

Learn approximately your home, in case you're a primary-generation college scholar, to help you get via the college enjoy. First-era-College-Students may additionally discover assets and guide services at many schools and institutions. Make certain to get yourself up to speed with and use those sources.

Speak together with your instructors. Your teachers may be a valuable supply of know-how and help. Attend your teachers' office hours and make certain to introduce your self.

Participate in Campus Life. A excellent approach to meet distinct students and experience part of the campus is to end up energetic inside the college network. You might also moreover furthermore participate in golf equipment and agencies, deliver lower lower returned to the community, or visit athletic sports and specific university-backed activities.

A first-generation college pupil also can find out it difficult to make friends, however it's miles in fact possible. By the usage of the above recommendation, you may make buddies, negotiate college existence, and connect with unique first-technology college college college students and current college college students.

Here are a few more guidelines for a first-era college scholar to make pals:

Be true. Avoid attempting to be someone you are not, that lets in you to wholesome in. When you act fake, others will be in a function to tell, and they will now not need to be round you as a extraordinary deal.

Be tolerant. Creating lasting friendships takes time. If you do no longer right now set up some of pals, strive no longer to come to be disheartened. Just maintain attractive within the subjects you need and putting yourself out there.

A splendid time! It need to be amusing to go to university. Enjoy your self and create a few great moments alongside aspect your new pals.

Making Friends as an LGBTQIA+ Student

Although it is probably hard, making pals as an LGBTQIA+-Student is actually possible. Hier are some advices:

Making buddies as an LGBTQIA+-Student might be hard.

LGBTQIA+-Students can also furthermore have the subsequent problems at the same time as forming friendships:

Apprehension of prejudice. Students who turn out to be aware of as LGBTQIA+ can be concerned approximately managing prejudice or harassment from their classmates, instructors, or different college employees. Being comfortable and making friends can be difficult as a give up end result.

Not being represented. Students who come to be privy to as LGBTQIA+ may additionally furthermore sense underrepresented in their Coursework or on Campus. They should experience by myself and lonely as a cease end result.

Microaggressions. Students who come to be aware of as LGBTQIA+ may additionally stumble upon minor slights from classmates, teachers, or certainly one of a type university personnel. Microaggressions are subtly offensive and separating sorts of prejudice.

Hints for interacting with heterosexual and LGBTQIA+-kids

Following are a few suggestions for meeting unique LGBTQIA+ and right away students:

Join scholar groups which might be LGBTQIA+. There are severa LGBTQIA+-Student-Groups in Colleges and Universities. These companies are notable belongings for connecting with LGBTQIA+ university students and growing a supportive network.

Attend courses with every heterosexual and LGBTQIA+ college students. Try, if you can, to join courses with both right now and LGBTQIA+ college students. It's a splendid chance to fulfill youngsters from all origins and discover different cultures.

Participate in after-college-sports activities activities. Participating in extracurricular activities is a tremendous way to make pals with distinctive youngsters, LGBTQIA+ and right away alike. You can also additionally volunteer for a purpose that topics to you or be a part of corporations and organizations which might be relevant on your hobbies.

Be inclined to have interaction with others. Don't be shy approximately making small chats and introductions to new human beings. Be curious to find out approximately the backgrounds and cultures of others.

Creating a Community that is constant and inviting

Creating a solid and accepting environment is vital for LGBTQIA+ university college students. You can cope with the issues of Discrimination and Harassment through having a safe and galvanizing surroundings, and it may also help you experience a part of your campus community.

Here are some recommendations for developing a Community that is constant and inspiring:

Join the LGBTQIA+ Center at your organization or college. Student assets and help are available in LGBTQIA+ Centers.

Make buddies with college college college students that perceive as LGBTQIA+. Students that discover as LGBTQIA+ can inspire you and assist you via your Difficulties.

Make friends with college students who are at once. You can increase ties with straight away university students and check right away tradition from right away university college college students.

Keep in touch collectively together with your native u.S.A.'s cherished ones and buddies. You could probably get emotional aid and motivation out of your buddies and family again domestic.

Although it might be tough, making pals as an LGBTQIA+-Student is certainly viable. You could make pals with LGBTQIA+ and right now university college students thru using the usage of the aforementioned recommendation, and you can create a community that is stable and inspiring.

Here are a few more pointers for LGBTQIA+ university college students on a way to make pals:

Be true. Avoid looking to be a person you are not, a good way to in shape in. When you act fake, others is probably in a role to inform, and that they might not want to be spherical you as masses.

Be tolerant. Creating lasting friendships takes time. If you do now not right away set up plenty of buddies, try no longer to turn out to be disheartened. Just keep appealing within the subjects you need and placing yourself available.

A extremely good time! It must be amusing to visit college. Enjoy yourself and create a few incredible moments together alongside your new buddies.

Keep in mind that you are not on my own. Many different LGBTQIA+ Kids try to set up buddies as nicely. You will in the long run find out your tribe, if you are open to meeting new people and are real.

## Chapter 6: Making Friends As A Veteran Student

It is probably hard to make friends as a pro student; however it's far very feasible.

Making pals as an skilled pupil is probably difficult.

Making friends might be difficult for seasoned university college students for some reasons:

Adjusting to Adulthood. It is probably hard to go from navy existence to civilian lifestyles. Veterans may additionally additionally enjoy uncomfortable in the college and can discover it hard to hook up with distinct college university college students, who've not long past through the identical testimonies as them.

In a super feel. Due to their navy backgrounds, veteran university students might also experience one-of-a-type from wonderful college students. They should have great opinions, life tales, and Ideals. It could be hard to connect with different scholars because of this.

lack of assist. Veterans won't get a good deal help from their cherished ones and pals lower back domestic. Making buddies and adjusting to university might be difficult as a give up result.

Advice on a way to have interaction with modern-day and former university students

Here are some guidelines for organising connections with current and previous college students:

Join seasoned collegiate corporations. Veteran scholar organizations are common at many Colleges and Institutions. These businesses are exceptional belongings for connecting with different skilled university college students and developing a supportive community.

Enroll in commands with modern-day students. Try to join courses with current university students, if the least bit possible.

It's a exquisite risk to get to apprehend existing students and discover the manner of life of the university.

Participate in after-faculty-sports activities sports. Participating in extracurricular sports activities is a incredible possibility to get to understand exquisite university students, every gift and previous. You may volunteer for a motive that subjects to you or be part of agencies and groups which might be relevant for your pastimes.

Be inclined to interact with others. Don't be shy about making small chats and introductions to new people. Be curious to find out about the backgrounds and cultures of others.

Getting used to civilian lifestyles

Get working on campus as a veteran student that will help you acclimate to civilian life. A brilliant method to fulfill unique college students and experience a part of your new community is to grow to be operating on campus. You also can participate in clubs and agencies, supply over again to the community, or visit athletic events and other college-sponsored sports.

Speak collectively with your instructors. Your instructors can be a valuable deliver of expertise and help. Attend your teachers' place of business hours and make sure to introduce yourself.

Use the facilities on the Campus. Veterans university university students may additionally moreover discover resources and useful resource programs at many colleges and establishments. Make excellent to make yourself familiar with and use the ones belongings.

It might be difficult to make friends as a seasoned pupil, but it's miles very feasible. By using the above advice, you can make near connections, connect with distinct professional and current college students, and adapt to each day lifestyles.

Here are a few greater guidelines for finding pals as an professional scholar:

Be proper. Avoid searching for to be someone you are not, to be able to match in. When you act fake, others can be succesful to inform, and that they'll no longer need to be spherical you as a good buy.

Be tolerant. Creating lasting friendships takes time. If you do now not right now set up pretty a few pals, try no longer to emerge as disheartened. Just maintain appealing inside the subjects you want and setting your self available.

A remarkable time! It must be amusing to visit college. Enjoy your self and create some incredible moments at the side of your new friends.

Keep in thoughts that you are not by myself. Many unique seasoned university students are likewise trying to establish pals. You will in the end discover your tribe, if you are open to meeting new humans and are actual.

Making Friends as a Mature Student

It is probably difficult to make pals as an older scholar, however it's far truely possible. Hier are some advices:

Making friends as a mature pupil might be tough.

Making friends might be hard for grownup college students for a few reasons:

In a unique revel in. Due to their age, Erfahrungen in lifestyles, and duties, mature university college students may also moreover experience now not like exceptional college students. They also can want to have extraordinary priorities, viewpoints, and values. It can be difficult to connect with different college students because of this.

Not sufficient time. Due to obligations to their households, jobs, and responsibilities, mature college college students may also moreover have heaps a whole lot much less time to socialize than Studenten. Building connections and meeting new humans may be hard as a end give up end result.

Fear of being rejected. Classmates which might be older can be terrified of being left out through more youthful classmates. Making new friends and setting oneself to be had may be difficult as a end result.

Hints for interacting with every more youthful and greater junior Kids

The following advice can help you have interaction with each older and younger university students:

Join businesses for older university college students. Student agencies are installed in masses of schools and universities. These agencies are fantastic locations to make buddies with special older college students and create a supportive community.

Attend commands with a numerous organization of university university college students. Try to join publications with college students of numerous a while, if in any respect feasible. It's a remarkable hazard to meet children from all origins and discover remarkable cultures.

Participate in after-college-sports activities. Participating in extracurricular activities is a notable opportunity to get to realise distinct university university college students, each older and greater younger college students. You may additionally volunteer for a motive that topics to you or be part of groups and corporations which are relevant to your interests.

Be inclined to interact with others. Don't be shy approximately making small chats and introductions to new human beings. Be curious to discover about the backgrounds and cultures of others.

organising connections with Individuals of each age

The Following are a few tips for growing connections with people of numerous some time:

Be actual. Avoid looking to be a person you aren't, for you to wholesome in. When you act faux, others can be in a position to tell, and they may not want to be round you as lots.

Be considerate. Be thoughtful of the mind and studies of others. Respect for others is possible, even if you disagree with them.

Take time to pay attention. When you supply someone some time and hobby, they will recognize it. Be curious about what the alternative person has to mention and ask questions.

Be encouraging. When your friends want you, be there for them. Support and inspire others.

It is probably difficult to make buddies as an older student, but it is virtually viable. The aforementioned recommendation will assist you interact with every older and younger college students and create connections with Individuals of all ages.

Here are a few more Preferences for grownup university college students on the manner to make friends:

Make the initial step with out hesitation. Approach all and sundry you note, who you will want to get to recognize, in case you see them. Don't preserve off, till they approach you.

Be tolerant. Creating lasting friendships takes time. If you do not without delay set up masses of pals, try not to emerge as disheartened. Just preserve attractive within the matters you want and putting your self to be had.

A extraordinary time! It have to be amusing to go to university. Enjoy your self and create some terrific moments along with your new pals.

Keep in mind that you are not by myself. There are numerous greater older college college students looking for to set up friends. You will in the end discover your tribe, in case you are open to meeting new humans and are genuine.

Making Friends as an Online Student

Although it is probably difficult, making buddies at the same time as reading online is genuinely practicable.

Making friends as a web pupil is probably hard.

Making buddies might be tough for online college students for a few motives:

Absence of face-to-face communication. Online university university college students do no longer have the identical possibilities as conventional college students to engage with their Professors and Classmates in character. Making buddies and forming connections may be challenging as a give up result.

Feeling by myself. Online newbies have to have a revel in of seclusion from every their pals and the larger faculty network. Diseases may be because of the absence of in-man or woman touch similarly to the ability global dispersion of on-line inexperienced people.

Not enough time. Due to duties to their families, jobs, and responsibilities, online university students may additionally additionally have lots much less time to socialize than conventional college university college students. Finding time to have interaction with wonderful students and form friendships may be hard as a surrender give up end result.

Advice for interacting with teachers and specific on line university college college students

## Chapter 7: Making Friends After Graduation

Although it is probably difficult, making friends after graduation is truely viable. Hier are some advices:

Making buddies after college is probably hard.

Making pals might be hard for smooth Grads for a few reasons:

A new city circulate. After commencement, many simple graduates relocate to a new area attempting to find employment or to preserve their have a look at. Building connections and meeting new humans can be difficult as a prevent stop result.

Opening a trendy function. It might in all likelihood take time and be difficult to begin a present day profession. It may be difficult to find the time and electricity to interact socially and increase new pals as a end result.

In a one among a kind experience. Because they're definitely beginning their jobs or because of the reality they've got now not however been married or given shipping to children, present day graduates may additionally experience specific from one of a kind Individuals in their age group. Finding not unusual ground and making pals is probably hard as a end result.

How to network with professionals and contemporary Grads

In order to community with other modern day grads and specialists, don't forget the following recommendation:

Join companies for professionals. Young Professionals Groups are set up in professional Organizations. Meet one of a kind latest grads and specialists to your subject through the ones organizations.

Go to networking gatherings. Building connections and meeting new people can also be completed within the route of networking sports. Industry activities, social activities, and volunteer sports activities sports are only a few examples of the numerous various sorts of networking activities.

Attend Seminars or Courses. Meeting new people and mastering new capabilities can be completed thru enrolling in seminars or workshops. At your network network college, an person training facility, or on line, you can sign up in courses or seminars.

Join a membership or agency for sports activities sports. Getting concerned with a sports crew or membership is a superb way to socialise and function fun. You can discover a sports activities sports team or club that hobbies you, considering the truth that there are such a variety of specific sorts.

The introduction of a state-of-the-art social community

The following advice will help you create a cutting-edge social community:

Be willing to engage with others. Don't be shy about making small chats and introductions to new people. Be curious to take a look at the backgrounds and cultures of others.

Be right. Avoid seeking to be a person you are not, as a way to suit in. When you act fake, others may be in a function to tell, and that they will now not need to be round you as masses.

Be encouraging. When your friends want you, be there for them. Support and encourage others.

Be considerate. Be thoughtful of the thoughts and reports of others. Respect for others is possible, even if you disagree with them.

Although it is probably difficult, making pals after commencement is in reality possible. You might also create a brand new social community and hook up with extraordinary contemporary grads and professionals with the useful resource of the use of the advice given above.

Following graduation, do not forget the subsequent greater recommendation for growing buddies:

Activate Social Media. Social Networking can be a incredible manner to fulfill new people and keep to preserve up a correspondence with contemporary friends. Social media may be used to come to be aware about golf equipment and sports activities that hobby you.

Attend Events. You may match to a massive kind of sports activities, which consist of live suggests, fairs, athletic events, and cultural events. Attending sports is a terrific manner to socialise and function fun.

Volunteer. Making a distinction to your network and assembly new people are great benefits of volunteering. You may additionally select out out a volunteer opportunity that appeals to you from maximum of the numerous which might be furnished.

Be tolerant. Creating lasting friendships takes time. If you do not right away establish masses of buddies, try no longer to grow to be disheartened. Just preserve enticing inside the things you like and putting yourself on hand.

Keep in thoughts that you aren't by myself. Similar to you, many particular sparkling grads are searching out Buddies. You will in the long run discover your tribe, in case you are open to meeting new people and are real.

## Chapter 8: Understanding The College Social Scene

College social landscape can be very difficult and worthwhile to navigate. A microcosm of civilization, it's far populated thru a large range of people from considered one of a type some time, ethnicities, cultures, and occupations. Building tremendous relationships starts offevolved offevolved offevolved with recognizing and valuing this distinction.

Diversity on Campus

One of the maximum awesome elements of university lifestyles is the variety you could come upon. From exceptional ethnicities and nationalities to severa notion structures and existence stories, the campus is a melting pot of views. Embracing this range may be an enriching revel in, as it opens doorways to new cultures, thoughts, and techniques of questioning. Engaging with people from severa backgrounds can growth your worldview and foster a more understanding of the worldwide network.

Identifying Different Social Circles

Within the wider university network, you could discover a myriad of social circles that cater to a significant kind of pursuits. These circles may additionally revolve spherical academic pursuits, shared interests, or cultural affiliations. Recognizing and appreciating the life of these circles permits you to explore in which you will possibly find your very own revel in of belonging. It's no longer about becoming into a predefined mildew, but as an alternative about coming across the spaces wherein your interests align with those of others.

Finding Like-Minded Individuals

While range is a cornerstone of the university experience, it is also vital to are looking for like-minded individuals who percent your passions and values. These are the individuals with whom you'll form deeper connections and potentially lifelong friendships. Whether it is thru a shared academic interest, a mutual love for a particular interest, or a common motive, finding people who resonate alongside aspect your aspirations can be profoundly desirable.

Remember, the university social landscape is dynamic and ever-evolving. It's no longer about conforming to a single mould, however about exploring the kaleidoscope of opportunities and connections to be had to you. Embrace the range, are seeking out for out your very personal social circles, and foster connections with folks who percent your passions. In doing so, you may lay the muse for a rich and satisfying college revel in.

Initiating Conversations

Starting conversations, specifically in a brand new surroundings like college, may be a effective manner to forge connections and assemble friendships. It's a capability that, once honed, can bring about enriching interactions and lasting relationships.

Icebreakers that Work

One of the simplest approaches to provoke a conversation is through the usage of icebreakers. These are verbal exchange starters designed to ease preliminary tensions and create a cushty ecosystem. A properly-selected icebreaker can variety from a clean assertion approximately the environment to sharing a relatable anecdote. Remember, the key's to be proper and approachable. By showing true hobby in others, you create a welcoming location for giant interplay.

Active Listening and Empathy

In any conversation, listening is simply as vital as speaking. Active listening includes not best paying attention to the phrases being said, but moreover know-how the emotions and intentions within the once more of them. It's about being gift inside the moment, giving your whole interest to the speaker, and displaying real interest in what they have got to say. Coupled with empathy, this office work the bedrock of deep and great connections. When you in reality pay attention and empathize, you're able to relate on a deeper degree, forging bonds that bypass beyond ground interactions.

Navigating Small Talk

Small communicate serves because the gateway to more extraordinary conversations. While it may seem superficial on the start, it is a crucial stepping stone toward constructing familiarity and take delivery of as real with. It's in these reputedly casual exchanges which you discover common floor and shared interests. Remember, small communicate want no longer be restrained to mundane topics; it could furthermore encompass discussions approximately commands, campus lifestyles, or maybe aspirations for the future. The key is to be proper and open, permitting the verbal exchange to glide in fact.

Initiating conversations is an art work that, like all abilities, improves with exercise. By using powerful icebreakers, actively listening, and showing empathy, you create a foundation for actual connections. Embrace small talk as a method to discover shared pursuits and pave the way for deeper conversations. In doing so, you may find that the relationships you gather in college may be a number of the maximum significant and enduring to your lifestyles.

## Getting Involved in Campus Activities

Active participation in campus sports activities is a cornerstone of the college experience. It offers a myriad of opportunities to not handiest pursue your pursuits however furthermore to connect with like-minded folks who share your passions.

## Joining Clubs and Organizations

Colleges are colorful hubs of severa pastimes, and becoming a member of clubs or businesses is a terrific way to immerse your self in a network that resonates with you. Whether it's miles a cultural membership, a sports activities activities sports institution, or an academic enterprise enterprise, the ones companies offer a space to have interaction with others who percentage your enthusiasm. It's internal those golf equipment that you will discover a supportive community of pals who can end up lifelong pals.

Attending Events and Workshops

Colleges are buzzing with a ordinary flow into of activities, workshops, and seminars. These gatherings offer a wealth of possibilities to increase your horizons and connect to fellow college college students. Whether it's a lecture with the useful resource of a remarkable traveller speaker or a arms-on workshop to your location of interest, attending such occasions may be a catalyst for every non-public and intellectual increase. Keep an eye fixed out for announcements and make it a issue to participate in activities that pique your hobby.

Volunteering Opportunities

Giving again to the network thru volunteering is not most effective a worthwhile assignment however additionally a effective manner to forge connections. Many schools have partnerships with community organizations or run their very own community business enterprise projects. This presents a platform if you want to engage with reasons you're passionate about, all whilst bonding with fellow college students who percent your strength of mind to making a great effect.

Remember, getting worried in campus sports isn't quite a good deal filling your time table; it's far about immersing yourself in reviews that resonate with you. It's approximately connecting with people who percentage your passions and values. By actively taking detail in golf equipment, attending sports, and giving once more via volunteering, you will discover that college will become a transformative adventure complete of substantial connections and personal increase.

## Chapter 9: Places To Locate Friends In Campus

When you display hobby in different human beings, you can create more friends in months than you can in years even as you attempt to expose hobby in others. — Dale Carnegie

Where I must visit meet prospective buddies is some aspect that I've previously had hassle identifying. Some humans may think that is obvious. However, having a particular list of locations is probably beneficial in case you're an introvert like myself while you recall that it may assist to lessen the uncertainty and tension round destiny contacts.

Even if you keep in mind yourself to be pretty sociable, you could not be aware of all of the venues you can go to in college an exceptional manner to fulfill people. When you supply it a few perception, in particular in case you attend a extremely good business corporation, it in all fairness absurd.

In order to help you find out pals at college, proper right here are 9 venues. Although now not an exhaustive list, that may be a brilliant location to begin. Please percentage any more locations you can bear in mind that I might also have not noted inside the feedback.

1. Campus Event

College is much like a 4-365 days TED or SXSW convention, in step with Thomas. This is seldom more glaring than in the course of university sports activities. At my college, the following have been just a few examples of the occurrences that often passed off:

unique website site visitors

creating a tune contests

Protests

charitable 5Ks

Craft evenings are loose.

activities including classical track

live overall performance series

Matches of TEDx Quidditch

themed dances (with complimentary meals!

Global Nomad social networks

The super way to make pals is in the course of campus activities. They cover the spectrum of consolation levels for extroverts and introverts, and they offer you an smooth speaking trouble (particularly if it is a few element like a speaker).

Learning approximately the ones sports has in no manner been less difficult way to Facebook. And take into account to take a look at the numerous posters that promote it they all at some stage in campus. There are probably occasions every night time of the week, so the actual hassle is choose which ones to wait.

Extra Hint: A reception is frequently held earlier than or after most activities, mainly people with visitor audio system. A communicate can be started out in the ones areas.

2. Campus organisation

Possibly the exceptional manner to satisfy humans is via campus organizations. Simply stated, this is because of their sheer numbers. There is virtually a club for a few trouble you're interested in, whether or now not it's far intramural sports activities, a social cause, a interest, music, or a venture.

In addition to meeting frequently, golf equipment revel in all of the advantages of campus sports activities. In order to increase friendships, it is crucial to have frequent encounters with the same people.

Reminder: Be selective on the equal time as deciding on your college groups. In the long term, it is better for your social life and strain levels to decide to 2-three groups which you really love and care approximately, even though it's OK to test out severa excellent clubs at the beginning of the semester.

The truth that excellent groups are better than others for making buddies is likewise vital to be aware. High-primarily based golf equipment, like a musical ensemble or the school council, can offer little region for individuals to in fact speak and get to understand each other.

That's now not to indicate that you should not be part of greater formal golf equipment (I emerge as in a couple of musical businesses in the course of college), but it is probably extra tough to establish pals in those settings than in less based ones like a walking club or a philosophy debate employer.

three. Classes

An whole week has 168 hours. That leaves you with 112 aware hours if you get preserve of an ok eight hours of sleep every night. Approximately 10.Seventy one% to thirteen.39% of your waking time is spent in splendor, which quantities to twelve to fifteen hours every week. A great danger to make buddies exists right right here.

For developing pals, certain publications are better than others, genuinely as with golf equipment. Even even though they may be frustrating, training with laboratories or organization initiatives often move higher given that they provide you greater possibility to have interaction with others than a lecture-best beauty.

Furthermore, commands gain surely from having a common hobby (or, no a whole lot less than, a shared duty, whether or not or no longer the class is well-known training or compulsory).

4. Your Dorm

Most possibly, you're to your dorm if you are not in beauty. Specially if it's miles your first yr in university. Dorms have one element going for them—they're an brilliant region to meet pals, however the terrible delicacies and the décor that seems like it modified into ripped from Doom. Even if it is most effective a common war that brings humans collectively.

The amount of unplanned social engagement that dormitories encourage makes them terrific, but. It's a incredible region to meet new people, whether or not or now not or no longer you are doing all of your schoolwork in the commonplace area, the usage of the restroom collectively, or having a spur-of-the-2nd Nerf battle within the hall at in the morning on a Tuesday.

Naturally, the aforementioned moreover holds actual for numerous sorts of habitation. I made a number of my satisfactory friends in college residing in a domestic with a collection of regularly random parents. Making an attempt to get to recognise your friends remains viable even in case you stay off campus in an rental.

five. Casual hangout

Large domestic occasions and competitive wreck tournaments in dorm lounges are also blanketed on this very big class. These regularly begin with an casual textual content like, "Hey, we need to all hold out tonight."

Nobody is aware of what is going to occur after that.

What's top notch approximately casual gatherings is that they provide you with lots of opportunity to virtually communicate with parents and get to understand them. (Okay, this will now not be actual if it is a wall-to-wall frat party blasting Kanye, but you get the issue).

In addition, due to the truth they may be casual, it is straightforward to go away if the state of affairs becomes uncomfortable. As may be referred to later, these varieties of gatherings are also wonderful for strengthening present day connections.

6. Campus Environment

Many human beings overlook approximately this, however if you have an open mind, you may come across a few quite exceptional dad and mom in this manner.

In essence, that is everywhere that is not class. A few times are:

The gymnasium—honestly, you have a commonplace interest if you're every workout.

The scholar center, that may be a extraordinary spot to start up a communicate and is amazing for people-watching.

organized in the corridor (whether or no longer or now not it's far in advance than beauty, in the course of a assembly with a professor, or for each one of a kind cause)

Walking approximately campus (glaringly, avoid being bizarre, but if you seem like going in the same direction or to the same location as a person, it genuinely is a super verbal exchange starter)

Due to the truth that it calls if you need to strike up a communicate with a stranger, this is without a doubt at the more "superior" diploma of making buddies. It's a remarkable technique to get over shyness, but, and boom yourself-warranty.

(7) Online

The most apparent manner to do this is with the resource of joining any Facebook groups related to your elegance or college. This may additionally additionally take many numerous shapes. While I did no longer interact on this hobby often myself, I knew folks that did so and have been capable of make friends in advance than the semester even started out out in reality by way of taking part inside the magnificence' Facebook page.

If, like me, you communicate more elegantly in writing than you do in man or woman, that is a notable direction of motion.

Simply avoid becoming a member of the organization spammers; it's now not cool.

## Chapter 10: Utilizing Common Spaces

Within the bustling environment of a university campus, common regions feature hubs of interaction, mastering, and rest. Knowing the way to successfully make use of these areas can significantly beautify your university enjoy.

The Library, Cafeteria, and Common Areas

The library, cafeteria, and terrific not unusual areas are greater than simply realistic areas; they'll be colourful social hubs. The library gives a serene environment for centered check durations and research, at the same time as the cafeteria offers a casual setting for mealtime conversations. These areas are high-quality for threat encounters and impromptu discussions. Make it a point to spend time in these regions, and do now not hesitate to strike up conversations with fellow college college students who proportion the ones areas with you.

Study Groups and Collaborative Learning

One of the great techniques to each analyze and make buddies in college is thru take a look at corporations and collaborative getting to know. These forums offer opportunities to exchange thoughts, tackle tough subjects, and deepen your know-how of coursework. They're additionally best for forming connections with classmates who percentage similar academic dreams and interests. Take the initiative to put together or be part of have a have a have a look at businesses; you may locate that the collective pursuit of understanding fosters great relationships.

Dormitory Socializing

Your dormitory is greater than in reality a place to sleep; it's far a network in itself. Dormitory socializing is an quintessential part of the university experience. Engage together with your dorm friends via shared sports activities, commonplace regions, and organized occasions. Establishing a experience of camaraderie internal your living surroundings can result in lasting friendships and a supportive community of friends.

Remember, those commonplace areas aren't honestly bodily places, however possibilities for connection. Embrace them as systems for interplay, collaboration, and relaxation. By doingso, you may discover that the college surroundings turns into a rich tapestry of studies and relationships that beautify your educational adventure and personal increase.

## ONLINE AND SOCIAL MEDIA NETWORKING

Online networking has grow to be a essential factor of college lifestyles in the digital era. Making the maximum of these structures may furthermore result in worthwhile relationships and profitable possibilities.

### Using Forums and Groups on Campus

Many establishments provide specific on line communicate boards or businesses in which university university college students can also participate in debates, trade statistics, and meet other like-minded students. These boards are troves of expertise and friendship. By actively accomplishing those online agencies, you can get right of entry to the mixture expertise and reviews of your university's scholar body. Don't be afraid to talk with exquisite university college students, percentage your thoughts, and ask questions.

Participating on Social Media Sites

Social media web sites are effective tool for installing vicinity connections with each your close by network and the relaxation of the globe. Being a part of university-unique Facebook or LinkedIn groups or pages may be a tremendous way to test possibilities, corporations, and sports on campus. Participate in conversations, percentage your very personal stories, and look for others who have comparable pursuits to you. Just keep in thoughts to behavior your self professionally and with respect on-line, as your virtual imprint may also have a large effect to your college profession and past.

Hangouts and digital have a look at durations

Virtual take a look at classes and hangouts have advanced into critical equipment for retaining social bonds and academic cooperation in an increasingly more associated society. Even even as you're bodily apart, structures like Zoom or Skype provide options for face-to-face conversation. To maintain a sense of network alive, installation on-line seminars, have casual hangouts, or sincerely prepare digital observe agencies. These on line exchanges can be actually as fruitful and first-rate as face-to-face encounters.

Embracing social media and online networking as critical components of your college enjoy offers up a international of possibilities for connection, teamwork, and improvement. You'll discover that the digital sphere can be a effective extension of your campus network via actively taking element in boards, the use of social media, and installing on line take a look at classes.

How to Manage Roommate Relationships

The collegiate revel in is extensively impacted through using dwelling with roommates. It takes open verbal exchange, understand for every different, and a desire to foster concord to efficiently navigate this dynamic.

Setting Expectations and Boundaries

It's critical to set up smooth limits and expectancies in conjunction with your roommate proper away. Talk about your opportunities for things like private space, visitors, and shared obligations like grocery purchasing and cleaning. An environment of recognize and consideration is constructed on an understanding of each special's desires and opportunities.

Communication limitations also are truly set up. Create a framework for discussing any troubles or capability troubles. This may include scheduled take a look at-ins or a duration set apart for candid conversations. You can also make sure that every elements enjoy heard and liked through manner of establishing a framework for verbal exchange.

Creating a Comfortable Living Space

A accurate university revel in calls for a supportive living state of affairs. Beyond physical comfort, this moreover consists of highbrow health. Encourage honest conversation and provide active interest to one another's problems. Express empathy and help, in particular in the route of trying instances.

A feeling of network also can be fostered with the aid of way of using taking element in shared sports or developing shared areas interior your living environment. Think about preparing food together, beautifying shared rooms, or organizing tours. These not unusual opinions can also additionally moreover deepen your connection and foster a sense of community.

Do now not forget about about that compromise and flexibility are essential. Giving and taking are critical whilst you percentage a area with someone. It's essential to be open to grievance and organized to alternate at the identical time as required.

In the surrender, healthy roommate relationships are based totally on mutual recognize, open communication, and a shared choice to create a welcoming living location. You can also moreover correctly address this part of university life by way of way of proactively setting limits and expectations in addition to through encouraging a experience of network.

Social gatherings and occasions to attend

Social gatherings and activities offer exciting possibilities to fulfill fantastic college college students and widen your social community. Making connections and forming prolonged-lasting friendships might also additionally get up even as you navigate these conferences with assure and sincerity.

Advice for Getting Around Parties

Be Prepared and Open-Minded: Approach social gatherings with a kind demeanor and a honest desire to make new friends. Take advantage of the risk to socialize.

Start with Small Talk: Ask quick, clean inquiries to begin discussions. Ask the other individual approximately their pastimes, publications, or reviews on college. This creates a comfortable surroundings for ongoing speak.

Active Listening: Concentrate on what different humans are saying. Building rapport entails intentionally responding and demonstrating hobby in their testimonies.

Seek for similar opinions or pastimes to find commonplace ground. It can be a shared elegance, a passion, or a not unusual upbringing. The basis of connection is locating factors of similarity.

Respect Personal Boundaries: Consider your comfort place and personal place. If a person makes a choice now not to participate in a advantageous problem or interest, continuously take delivery of their preference.

Avoid Abundant Alcohol Use: If alcohol is worried, restrict your consumption. Controlling your talents permits greater pleasant and proper encounters.

Introduce Yourself: Don't be shy approximately drawing near groups or humans you need to get to apprehend. A honest greeting and a smile may work a long manner.

Building Connections in a Social Setting

Building connections at social sports entails greater than surely casual verbal exchange. It's approximately forming proper bonds with others. Remember names and information about the humans you meet. Follow up with them after the occasion, probable suggesting a have a take a look at consultation or a casual get-together.

Additionally, don't forget web hosting your personal social events. This gives an possibility to supply humans together in a setting you are comfortable with, permitting you to foster connections in an surroundings that suits you.

Ultimately, attending social sports and sports is an essential a part of the university revel in. By coming close to those gatherings with authenticity, active listening, and a willingness to construct connections, you may locate that they turn out to be valuable possibilities for private increase and friendship.

## Chapter 11: Balancing Academics And Social Life

Achieving stability amongst instructors and social life is a crucial component of the university enjoy. It requires effective time manipulate, prioritization, and a conscious approach to every non-public and educational increase.

Time Management and Prioritization

Mastering time manage is essential to locating equilibrium among your educational duties and your social existence. Start via developing a based time table that allocates unique time slots for education, have a study lessons, and extracurricular sports. Prioritize assignments based totally on last dates and complexity, ensuring which you allocate sufficient time for each. Remember to moreover allocate time for self-care, rest, and social interactions. Striking this balance empowers you to excel academically at the identical time as moreover playing a satisfying social life.

## Study Groups as Social Opportunities

Study businesses offer a totally unique intersection of tutorial manual and social interplay. They provide a platform for collaborative getting to know and the change of mind. Beyond their instructional benefits, study groups additionally foster camaraderie amongst human beings. Engage actively in the ones training, now not simplest to beautify your understanding of the fabric however moreover to form connections along with your friends. By combining the pursuit of instructional excellence with social interplay, you are able to domesticate relationships that amplify past the classroom.

Remember, it is not about sacrificing one element for the other; as an alternative, it is approximately finding harmony a few of the two. Embrace the mission of balancing lecturers and social existence as an possibility for personal increase and holistic development.

## Dealing with Rejections and Setbacks

In the journey of making pals and navigating university life, rejections and setbacks are an inevitable part of the system. Learning a manner to deal with those stressful situations is a crucial potential that fosters private growth and resilience.

## Understanding that Rejections are Common

It's critical to understand that experiencing rejections is a normal element of life. Whether in social interactions, academic pursuits, or private endeavors, setbacks are an inherent part of the human experience. Understanding that everybody faces rejection at some point allows normalize the ones opinions. It's not a reflected picture of your absolutely nicely well worth or capabilities, but as an alternative a natural a part of the mastering manner.

## Building Resilience and Moving Forward

Resilience is the functionality to get higher from disappointments and setbacks. Cultivating this trait empowers you to stand stressful situations with a excessive first-class outlook and an unwavering willpower to persevere. Here are some techniques to construct resilience:

Practice Self-Reflection: Take time to mirror on the state of affairs. Analyze what went wrong and what you could studies from the enjoy.

Maintain a Growth Mindset: Embrace setbacks as possibilities for increase. See them as stepping stones within the route of private improvement and self-development.

Seek Support: Don't hesitate to lean to your help network. Friends, family, or campus assets can offer precious perspective and encouragement.

Set Realistic Expectations: Understand that now not every interplay or mission will yield the preferred final results, and that is perfectly normal. Adjust your expectations consequently.

Focus on What You Can Control: Direct your strength in the direction of components you've got got were given have an effect on over, in preference to living on matters past your manage.

Engage in Self-Care: Prioritize your physical and emotional properly-being. Engage in sports activities activities that rejuvenate your spirit and offer a sense of stability.

Celebrate Small Wins: Recognize and feature a very good time your achievements, irrespective of how small. Acknowledging progress, however incremental, boosts your self notion and motivation.

Remember, setbacks are not indicative of your properly really worth or capacity for achievement. They are opportunities for growth and gaining knowledge of. By knowledge that rejections are commonplace, and with the resource of the usage of constructing resilience thru self-mirrored photo and self-care, you may emerge from those opinions more potent and further organized to face future traumatic conditions.

## Building Long-lasting Friendships

Creating enduring friendships is a rewarding and essential issue of the university experience. These connections frequently end up a cornerstone of your private and expert existence.

## Deepening Connections

Investing time and effort into your friendships is crucial for their sturdiness. Actively concentrate, display empathy, and be determined on your interactions. Share evaluations and assist one another via each triumphs and disturbing conditions. By deepening your connections, you domesticate relationships that stand the test of time.

## Nurturing Friendships Beyond College

As graduation techniques, it is herbal to wonder how your friendships will evolve. The key's to make intentional efforts to preserve and nurture the ones relationships. Stay in contact via normal communique, plan reunions or meetups, and be there for each distinctive in instances of need. Shared history and mutual aid are the regulations of friendships that go through past university.

## Chapter 12: Understanding Introversion

In a global wherein extroverts frequently steal the spotlight like overenthusiastic magicians pulling rabbits out of hats, it's time to shine a light at the subtle magic of introversion. If the extravert is the existence of the birthday celebration, then the introvert is the snug corner in the corner wherein the partygoer goes to locate their out of place keys (and possibly a second of serenity).

Introversion isn't about being a recluse or a hermit with a prolonged, scraggly beard (regardless of the truth that, if that's your style, circulate for it). No, introverts are just like the connoisseurs of life who choose sipping a pleasant wine of solitude in a global captivated with chugging social snap shots on the bar of steady interplay. Now, buckle up, my fellow introvert, as we every embark in this journey to locate the quirks, strengths, and mystery superpowers of introversion, all at the identical time as sharing a know-how, introvert-style wink with our fellow wallflowers.

What Is Introversion?

Our international in an area wherein extroversion often takes center level, like a thoughts-blowing Broadway show with all its charismatic characters and lively melodies, introversion quietly lingers inside the wings, looking beforehand to its 2d to shine. Imagine, if you can, a grand spectrum of human personalities, in which extroverts gleam brightly much like the blazing solar, radiating power and drawing others into their orbit. In this spectrum, introverts possess the moderate, airy glow of the moon, casting a smooth, reflective moderate upon the area.

Introversion isn't someone flaw or a timid retreat from social interaction; it's a completely unique and captivating trait that shapes how we understand and engage with the area around us. If extroverts thrive in the bustling electricity of a carnival, introverts discover solace inside the calm of a moonlit seaside, in which the rhythmic waves whisper stories most effective they might pay attention. It's essential to apprehend that introversion isn't a deficiency; it's a completely unique lens thru which we view and navigate life.

I will such as you to photograph a serene night, with a cosy blanket wrapped round your shoulders and your chosen e-book cradled to your palms. Each phrase is a treasure, every internet internet web page a portal to each specific international. In this 2d, you're no longer by myself; you're inside the organisation of the characters and the writer's thoughts, and it's a symphony of solitude that fills your soul. This is the essence of introversion—an capability to get pleasure from the richness of solitary research.

Or permit your imagination wander to a tranquil wooded area, in which the air is thick with the earthy perfume of moss and the cover overhead creates a inexperienced cathedral. The rustling of leaves is your symphony, and the songs of birds are your partners. In the heart of this natural haven, you discover a profound connection to the vicinity round you. Here, surrounded via the tranquil encompass of nature, introverts often find out their spirits invigorated.

Introverts, no longer like extroverts, draw their energy from indoors. It's as despite the fact that they have got a wellspring of electricity deep of their souls that flows once they engage in introspection, creativity, or quiet contemplation. Large gatherings and raucous events, whilst fun fairly, can quick expend their inner reserves. Social interactions, mainly with unexpected faces, can feel like siphoning fuel from a vehicle's fuel tank. It's now not that introverts dislike people; it's that they require moments of solitude to refuel, regroup, and reconnect with themselves.

But allow's remedy a time-venerated false impression: introverts are not synonymous with shyness or anti-social dispositions. Shyness relates greater to social anxiety—a fear of judgment or horrible evaluation in social conditions. Introverts can be outgoing, sociable, and first rate communicators. They have the functionality to interact in charming conversations, percentage laughter, and hook up with others on a deep, massive degree. The key distinction lies in how they recharge—introverts accomplish that through moments of quiet reflected photo and introspection, while extroverts frequently benefit strength from being in the organization of others.

So, if you're picturing an introvert as a recluse hiding away in a dusty attic, writing melancholic poetry with the aid of using candlelight, it's time to rethink that stereotype. Introverts are everywhere, whether or no longer they're engrossed in a lively speak with close to buddies, immersed in an artwork studio developing masterpieces, or surely playing a solitary walk in the park. They stroll amongst us, their introverted superpowers frequently hidden below the surface.

The Strengths of Introverts

In a international that looks to venerate the loud and the extroverted, it's time to drag decrease again the curtain and shine a spotlight at the frequently-omitted strengths of introverts. Picture introversion as a treasure chest of competencies, a hidden superpower truely ready to be unleashed upon the arena. While extraverts may moreover furthermore command the diploma with their boisterous presence, introverts wield their power with a quiet, profound finesse.

One of the hallmarks of introverts is their propensity for deep wondering. Like divers exploring the ocean's depths, introverts plunge into the intricacies of thoughts and ideas. While others may additionally skim the floor, introverts dig deeper, unearthing the buried treasures of records and notion. We're the ones who mull over the "what ifs" and "whys" extended after the conversation has moved on to lighter subjects. It's in the ones quiet moments of contemplation that introverts frequently discover profound insights and innovative solutions which have the functionality to reshape the area.

But that's now not all; introverts have an innate skills for listening that extends far beyond the superficial change of phrases. When an introvert listens, it's no longer absolutely with their ears; it's with their hearts and minds. We choose up at the diffused shifts in tone, the hidden emotions, and the unspoken narratives that weave via conversations. It's as although we very own a finely tuned emotional radar, allowing us to hook up with others on a deeper, greater actual diploma. This functionality to certainly pay attention and recognize the ones round us makes introverts the pass-to confidants, depended on buddies who provide a secure harbor for secrets and techniques and vulnerabilities.

Perhaps one of the maximum fascinating additives of introversion is the way it nurtures creativity. While extroverts may additionally draw idea from the colorful chaos of social interactions, introverts find their muse within the quiet corners of their non-public minds. It's within this tranquil sanctuary that creativeness blooms, unfettered through the usage of outside distractions. Introverts are the poets who craft verses that seize the essence of human emotion, the artists who translate their inner landscapes onto canvas, and the inventors who dream up groundbreaking mind at some point of solitary moments of mirrored image. Some of history's maximum celebrated creators, from writers like J.K. Rowling and George Orwell to scientists like Albert Einstein, have worn the badge of introversion proudly as they harnessed their inner worlds to form fact.

When it involves problem-solving, introverts have an arsenal of competencies at their disposal. Armed with a considerate, analytical mind-set, they approach demanding conditions with a completely particular aggregate of precision and creativity. While extroverts may additionally additionally rely upon speedy-fireplace brainstorming durations, introverts prefer to marinate in the hassle, analyzing it from every mind-set like a jeweler scrutinizing a precious gem. This meticulous technique frequently consequences in unconventional, yet remarkably powerful answers. Moreover, introverts excel in enterprise settings, wherein their capability to synthesize thoughts and promote collaboration shines brightly. They're the glue that holds severa companies collectively, making sure that every voice is heard and each mind-set is considered, ultimately essential to greater sturdy and revolutionary consequences.

Common Introvert Misconceptions

In the grand theater of personalities, introverts have extended been assigned roles that don't quite in shape. It's time to roll once more the curtains and dispel the misconceptions which have shrouded introversion in a fog of misconception. These misconceptions, like cussed specters, grasp-out the way human beings perceive introverts. Let's get to the lowest of them one after the other.

1. Misconception 1: Aloofness and Unfriendliness

If you've ever determined an introvert in a social placing, you may probably have fallacious their quiet demeanor for aloofness or unfriendliness. It's a not unusual misconception that introverts are standoffish or cold. But the truth is pretty the alternative.

Introverts aren't antisocial; they're selectively social. Think of it this way: if socializing had been a buffet, introverts can be the ones cautiously selecting their preferred dishes in preference to piling the whole thing onto their plate. We're like nice wines that want time to respire and display our whole flavor.

When you first meet an introvert, you can discover them reserved, probably even a chunk shy. But below that preliminary layer of reticence lies a international of heat, kindness, and companionship. Introverts are like coiled springs, prepared to unleash their actual selves once they sense cushty on your presence. We won't be the lifestyles of the birthday celebration, however we're the friend who'll pay attention to your woes, provide sage advice, and keep in mind your birthday at the same time as not having a Facebook reminder.

So, the following time you come upon an introvert who appears aloof within the starting appearance, offer them the existing of time and endurance. You'll be rewarded with a devoted pal who values the intensity of connection over superficiality.

2. Misconception 2: Disliking Socializing

Another false impression that wants to be tossed out the window is the notion that introverts don't experience socializing. This one is as an extended manner from the fact as believing that a cat doesn't enjoy a comfortable sunbeam nap. Introverts do enjoy social interaction, but carefully and on their very very own terms.

Picture this: even as extroverts may also thrive in the bustling strength of a crowded party, introverts often discover solace in quieter gatherings or great one-on-one conversations. It's not approximately maintaining off social conditions; it's approximately savoring them like a great dessert in location of devouring the entire buffet.

Introverts charge high-quality over amount of their social interactions. We cherish the deep connections solid thru real conversations, wherein mind and emotions are shared brazenly. But right right here's the twist—social exhaustion is a actual battle for introverts. After a energetic accumulating or an afternoon filled with meetings, we need time to recharge our internal batteries. It's like our social strength bar depletes faster than that of our extroverted counterparts.

So, at the same time as you invite an introvert to a gathering, don't be discouraged inside the event that they sometimes decline or slip away early. It's now not a rejection; it's their way of keeping a touchy equilibrium amongst socializing and keeping their mental and emotional well-being.

three. Misconception three: Passivity and Lack of Assertiveness

Introverts are frequently pegged as passive those who lack assertiveness. The photo that could come to mind is of a person who fades into the heritage, in no way voicing their thoughts or evaluations. But this stereotype couldn't be in addition from the fact.

Introverts can be reserved, however it's a misconception to equate quietness with passivity. We have thoughts, insights, and reviews as wealthy and precious as every person else's. The difference lies in our method to communique.

When introverts communicate, they acquire this with purpose. We choose out out our phrases cautiously, aiming for precision and intensity in choice to filling the air with pointless chatter. In enterprise discussions, introverts frequently concentrate attentively, processing statistics in advance than presenting well-considered contributions.

The world can also need to gain from records that introverts' quiet power lies in their functionality to foster considerate speak and collaboration. They excel at synthesizing mind and mediating disputes with grace and poise. It's like having a keep close chess participant for your organization, quietly plotting the precise movements while others interact in noisy skirmishes.

In the place of job, introverts may be strategic thinkers, hassle solvers, and powerful leaders. Their calm and contemplative technique regularly yields progressive solutions and promotes a harmonious paintings environment. So, don't underestimate the strength of an introvert's voice; when they communicate, it's frequently truely really worth taking note of.

4. Misconception four: Introverted Professions and Hobbies

The very last false impression we'll cope with is the idea that introverts are sincerely interested by introverted professions and pursuits, which incorporates writing, portray, or solitary scientific research. While it's real that many introverts find out solace in those interests, it's a mistake to anticipate that introverts are constrained to unique profession paths or interests.

Introversion isn't always a vocational sentence—it's a individual trait which could beautify one's standard performance in any place. It's now not about what you do; it's about the way you do it. Introverts can thrive in extroverted professions, alongside facet income, marketing, or public speaking, through leveraging their particular strengths, like active listening, empathy, and thoughtful verbal exchange.

In reality, introverts often bring a clean mindset to collaborative endeavors. They encourage deeper exploration of thoughts and offer balance in group dynamics. It's like having a seasoned navigator on a deliver, making sure that the adventure is well-charted and thoughtful of all viewpoints.

When it involves interests, introverts may also moreover moreover revel in sports that permit them to tap into their inner worlds, however they will be in no way constrained to solitary interests. Introverts can be placed trekking in nature, undertaking agency sports activities sports, or participating in employer art work duties. It's all about finding the proper balance amongst solitude and social engagement, regardless of one's private pursuits.

Embracing Your Introversion

Welcome to the area of introversion, wherein the quiet ones keep their very private precise sort of magic. To surely embody your introversion is to embark on a adventure of self-discovery and self-recognition. It's about spotting the excellent symphony that is your introverted self and learning how to dance to its quiet, melodious song. So, dirt off your introvert cape and permit's find out the enchanted woodland of introversion collectively.

Find Your Sanctuary

First matters first, each introvert needs a sanctuary. Think of it as your private Batcave or your Hogwarts Common Room. It's the area wherein you could retreat whilst the arena feels a piece too noisy. Maybe it's a comfortable reading nook in which you may immerse your self within the worlds of your preferred books. Perhaps it's a serene lawn wherein you can lose yourself within the mild rustle of leaves. It should additionally be that corner café with the high-quality environment for deep thoughts.

In your sanctuary, you recharge like a superhero. It's wherein you shed the layers of social interplay and allow your introverted soul breathe. Here, you're unfastened to be your real self, with out a judgment or expectancies. So, discover that sanctuary and visit it regularly, for it is your introverted citadel of solitude.

Nurture Your Interests

Introverts are frequently passionate beings. We dive deep into the rabbit holes of our pastimes, exploring them with the ardour of a treasure hunter uncovering historic artifacts. It is probably a fascination with astrophysics, an obsession with vintage vinyl facts, or an insatiable love for baking difficult pastries.

Whatever your ardour, nurture it like a sensitive flower. Water it with understanding, daylight hours it with practice, and watch it bloom into a top notch garden of know-how.

These hobbies are not sincerely interests; they may be the essence of your introverted soul. They're the threads that weave the tapestry of your existence.

When you have got interplay together together with your passions, you're no longer in reality passing time; you're living with purpose. You're tapping into that introverted well of creativity and imagination that gadgets you aside. So, don't be afraid to permit your pastimes flourish. They are the colours that make your introverted canvas colorful.

Cultivate Meaningful Connections

Contrary to the lone-wolf stereotype, introverts crave connection as loads as every person else. However, we decide on tremendous over quantity close to relationships. We trying to find the kindred spirits who recognize the language of silence and the splendor of depth. These are the those who recognize your authenticity and cherish your introspective nature.

In the vicinity of introversion, friendships are like aged satisfactory wine. They take time to mature and deepen. So, be affected individual for your quest for awesome connections. Don't be discouraged thru the cacophony of small speak; the actual symphony of friendship lies in the conversations that discover the depths of your mind and feelings.

Surround yourself with buddies who now not first-class take transport of your want for solitude however have a good time it. These are the buddies who might be a part of you in stargazing on a quiet night time time time, sipping tea in companionable silence, or embarking on epic adventures via the pages of a book. They are your fellow introverted vacationers in this adventure of lifestyles.

2THE COLLEGE TRANSITION

The first two weeks at college were a whirlwind of feelings, expectations, and a enjoy of trepidation that regarded to grasp to me like an invisible shroud. As I stepped onto the campus, it felt like I had entered a bustling city of strangers. The sea of unexpected faces and the cacophony of conversations made my coronary coronary coronary heart race with each exhilaration and tension.

For a person like me, an introvert through nature, this transition became an exceptional undertaking. The weight of social interactions and the fear of judgment loomed over me like a storm cloud. Making friends had generally been a struggle, and the chance of doing so on this new surroundings felt like an insurmountable project.

The first day on campus have become a blur of orientation events and icebreaker activities. Everyone seemed to outcomes introduce themselves, trade cellular phone numbers, and form instantaneous connections. I, then again, stood at the periphery, a silent observer in a global that felt distant places and overwhelming.

My dormitory room became my sanctuary in the course of these preliminary days. It become a cocoon of solitude wherein I must retreat from the constant buzz of social interplay. While my roommate eagerly ventured out to fulfill new human beings, I determined solace inside the comfort of my thoughts and the familiarity of my books.

The consuming hall changed into a battleground of tension. The belief of drawing near a desk complete of strangers and placing up a communication sent shivers down my backbone. I often observed myself consuming by myself, my gaze consistent on a ebook or a notepad as a guard against the loneliness that threatened to engulf me.

As the times changed into weeks, the weight of isolation grew heavier. I yearned for connection, for a person to understand the thoughts that swirled inner me. The silence in my room started out to sense suffocating, and the empty seats at the cafeteria appeared like a stark reminder of my loss of potential to interrupt via the limitations of introversion.

I watched with envy as my fellow college students resultseasily shaped bonds. They laughed, shared reminiscences, and embarked on adventures collectively. It come to be as in spite of the reality that I emerge as a spectator in a movie, longing to be part of the colorful scene in advance than me. But each time I tried to sign up for a communique, my words stumbled, my heart raced, and I retreated into my self-imposed cocoon of silence.

Loneliness settled in like an unwelcome traveler. It changed into a regular accomplice during those first weeks, a shadow that observed me anywhere I went. I careworn my simply well worth and my potential to suit into this new international. The worry of rejection gnawed at me, stopping me from taking the dangers required to forge new connections.

The lectures and coursework provided a quick distraction, however they couldn't fill the void of companionship. While I excelled academically, my social existence remained stagnant. I longed for someone to percentage my triumphs and setbacks with, to discover the campus, and to embark at the adventures that university existence promised.

It become at some point of 1 particularly lonely night, as I sat in my dimly lit dorm room, that a profound popularity washed over me. I couldn't allow my introversion define my college enjoy. I needed to take manage of my narrative and embark on a journey of self-discovery and boom.

And so, the transformation started. I started with small, courageous steps. I attended campus sports activities, even if it meant pushing past my comfort vicinity. I pressured myself to initiate conversations with fellow college university students, slowly analyzing the paintings of small communicate and energetic listening.

I moreover sought solace inside the splendor of campus. The sprawling lawns, the quiet corners of the library, and the serene paths through the river have become my sanctuaries. These were locations wherein I should discover moments of solitude and recharge my introverted spirit.

As the weeks handed, I commenced to see glimmers of exchange. I met folks that appreciated my thoughtful nature and my functionality to pay hobby. I found shared interests and passions that served as bridges to forming connections. And, most significantly, I positioned out that being an introvert become no longer a susceptible point but a unique aspect of my identity.

The first weeks at university were honestly tough, marked by means of using isolation and self-doubt. But they had been moreover the catalyst for a adventure of self-discovery and transformation. It have end up a reminder that introverts, too, may want to thrive inside the international of college, armed with resilience and a willingness to encompass boom.

Entering college is just like stepping into a whole new global—a world teeming with possibilities, traumatic conditions, and a sense of newfound independence. For introverts like me, this transition wasn't only a alternate of surroundings; it have become a seismic shift in my lifestyles. This financial catastrophe of my adventure into making buddies in university as an introvert delves into the intricacies of this pivotal period, and it all starts offevolved offevolved with steerage.

Preparing for College Life: Embracing the Unknown

Preparing for university life is just like making ready for an excursion into the unknown, an adventure that beckons with the promise of self-discovery and new horizons. Yet, as a younger introvert, this coming near transformation modified into now not quite a good deal selecting what clothes to % or which books to take alongside; it changed into a adventure of profound self-mirrored picture, introspection, and a careful exam of my identification.

Leaving the cocoon of my uncle's domestic modified into both a momentous and daunting challenge. It modified right into a departure from the acquainted, from the reassuring physical activities that had described my life so far. Venturing right into a dorm room full of strangers, each bearing their private hopes, goals, and memories, felt like stepping onto a tightrope suspended excessive above a global of uncertainties.

The days most crucial as much as my departure have been full of a whirlwind of emotions. There changed into pleasure, of path, a sense of pleasure at the possibility of newfound independence and the adventures that awaited me. Yet, under that pleasure, there has been an undercurrent of hysteria, the type that accompanies the uncharted territories of existence.

Practicality demanded interest. Packing suitcases, organizing documents, and selecting the necessities have been obligations that required meticulous making plans. Every item selected to accompany me in this voyage carried a weight of importance, representing now not definitely physical necessity however moreover the emotional luggage I have become about to embark upon.

But beyond the tangible elements of practise lay a deeper, more profound layer. It end up a layer of mental and emotional readiness, an information that college modified into no longer quite a exquisite deal lectures and textbooks however approximately private increase and discovery. It modified into about accepting that it become flawlessly adequate to be an introvert, that my precise perspective, my propensity for introspection, and my penchant for quiet contemplation had been valuable belongings to carry with me in this journey.

The system of packing a mind-set started with introspection. I launched right right into a voyage of self-discovery, delving deep into my mind and emotions. I sought to understand now not most effective what I desired from this new financial disaster in my life but moreover who I become as an character. What had been my strengths? What had been my weaknesses? What had been the values that defined me, and the way ought to they guide me in this uncommon terrain?

In the quiet moments of introspection, I decided that being an introvert grow to be no longer a disadvantage however a totally specific trouble of my identity. My inclination for solitary interests, my capability to pay attention keenly, and my ability for deep reflection were characteristics that might serve me nicely inside the pursuit of information and the formation of big connections.

As I packed my thoughts-set, I observed out that my introversion turned into now not some detail to be conquer but a few aspect to be embraced. It become part of who I turn out to be, an intrinsic thread in the tapestry of my being. Instead of viewing it as a hurdle, I began out to look it as a supply of strength, a wellspring of resilience that might empower me to navigate the demanding situations of university lifestyles.

Equipped with this newfound attitude, I set approximately putting realistic dreams. I understood that the transition to college need to not be without its trials. It changed right into a terrain marked thru uncertainty, complete of tutorial disturbing situations, and steeped inside the complexities of social interplay. However, I changed into determined no longer to allow these stressful situations crush me.

My desires were grounded in realism. I mentioned that there might be moments of self-doubt and loneliness. There may be instances at the equal time as the unfamiliarity of the environment might appear overwhelming. But I moreover identified that those moments were part of the journey, opportunities for growth as opposed to insurmountable obstacles.

One of my primary goals changed into to keep my authenticity. I vowed no longer to succumb to societal pressures or expectancies that suggested me to be a person I wasn't. I favored to embody my introverted nature, to enjoy the moments of solitude that allowed me to recharge and replicate. I knew that only with the beneficial aid of staying authentic to myself may additionally additionally need to I desire to form proper connections with others.

Another purpose turned into to actively are seeking for out like-minded folks who shared my pastimes and passions. I understood that finding kindred spirits may be a catalyst for friendship and personal increase. So, I researched golf equipment and companies that aligned with my interests, making sure that I ought to have opportunities to connect with folks that shared my values.

As the day of departure drew nearer, I couldn't assist however feel a combination of anticipation and tension. The path ahead was nevertheless shrouded in uncertainty, but I had packed my attitude with resilience and reputation. I knew that the university adventure could be a transformative one, complete of moments of self-discovery and boom.

Leaving the cocoon of my uncle's domestic modified into no longer simplest a physical transition; it changed into a change of the soul. It have end up a reputation that the tour into the unknown became now not a solitary one but a collective adventure shared through limitless others, every with their very non-public hopes, desires, and fears.

Navigating Campus Culture: Embracing the Labyrinth of Diversity

Stepping onto the university campus for the number one time become similar to entering into every different international—an intricately woven tapestry of people, opinions, and cultures. Each corner of the campus became a portal to a cutting-edge journey, and for an introvert like me, it felt like decoding an enigmatic code that held the critical aspect to belonging.

The variety of campus way of existence modified proper right into a double-edged sword, a thrilling and intimidating prospect. The student body changed into a mosaic of backgrounds, hobbies, and personalities, a microcosm of the sector itself. As I placed my fellow college students bustling about, I couldn't help but feel like an outsider looking at up at the night time sky, in which cliques shaped constellations, every with its personal set of stars.

In the ones initial days, the worry of social judgment loomed huge. The idea of venturing into the unknown, of coming near strangers with awesome research and views, sent tremors of tension through my introverted soul. The challenge end up daunting: how ought to I, an introvert, navigate this tough internet of relationships and find out my location inside it?

But quick, I came to realize that beneath the ground of variety lay a lovely reality—university culture was no longer a monolith. It changed into, in reality, a tapestry of character memories, waiting to be woven together. And so, my journey of navigating campus life-style started out, marked with the useful resource of a sequence of revelations and changes.

Exploring the Constellations of Cliques

One of the primary training I determined out changed into that cliques, those constellations within the social night time sky, were no longer impenetrable galaxies. They have been fashioned with the aid of folks who shared commonplace interests and affinities, and the beauty of university modified into that there has been a constellation for in truth all people.

With hobby as my compass, I began out attending severa campus sports. From paintings exhibitions to astronomy club conferences, I explored the myriad of possibilities. These activities have been like cosmic gateways, each presenting a danger to engage with folks that shared my passions and values.

At an paintings exhibition, I met fellow introverts who determined solace in the brushstrokes of a canvas and the beauty of silent contemplation. In the astronomy membership, I encountered individuals whose fascination with the cosmos pondered my very very own, and we spent countless nights beneath the celebrities, our introverted spirits hovering amidst the constellations.

The Art of Small Talk and Active Listening

Navigating campus tradition additionally supposed analyzing the paintings of conversation. As an introvert, small communicate had continually been a powerful adversary. But I quickly observed out that it modified into a bridge to deeper connections. I launched right right into a quest to decipher the nuances of human interplay.

I decided the extroverted stars of our campus, people who effects lit up rooms with their air of mystery. What I found modified into that they, too, had once been novices in the global of socializing. They had honed their skills thru exercise, and so may additionally want to I.

I started via the usage of asking open-ended questions, the keys that unlocked meaningful conversations. I positioned out to pay attention, in reality listen, now not honestly to the terms but to the emotions and stories within the lower back of them. Active listening have end up my superpower, allowing me to connect on a profound degree.

The Oasis of Solitude

While navigating campus lifestyle have grow to be approximately embracing range and forging connections, it emerge as further important to preserve my introverted nature. I understood that I desired moments of solitude to recharge, to reflect, and to live real to myself.

The bustling campus had its hidden oases of solitude. The library, with its rows of books whispering knowledge, have become my sanctuary. There, amidst the pages of novels and the hushed reverence of fellow college students, I determined solace.

The river that wound through our campus end up some other safe haven. Its tranquil banks supplied an area of stillness, a area in which I need to retreat from the constant hum of social interplay and immerse myself inside the melody of flowing water.

Balancing the need for connection with the want for solitude became an paintings I had to master. It have become a dance the diverse colourful tapestry of campus existence and the quiet moments of introspection that stored me grounded.

The Realization of Unity in Diversity

As the weeks grow to be months, a change commenced to take form. I turn out to be no longer the timid observer on the sidelines of campus manner of life; I had turn out to be an active participant. I had woven my very very own constellation inside the tapestry, fashioned of buddies who celebrated my introverted nature and favored the intensity of our interactions.

What I had as quickly as perceived as an intimidating labyrinth of range had end up a supply of idea and growth. I had encountered individuals from all walks of lifestyles, each with their precise story to tell. These reminiscences had stepped forward my horizons, shattered stereotypes, and ignited my interest.

Navigating campus way of lifestyles had taught me that introverts, too, had a place in the colourful mosaic of college life. It changed into an area wherein introversion changed into not a quandary however a completely particular attitude to be celebrated. My introverted nature, with its penchant for introspection and empathy, had enriched my connections and allowed me to look the splendor in the sort of human reviews.

Managing Academic Stress: Navigating the Storm

The transition from excessive university to college marked a great shift in my instructional adventure, one that introduced with it the tempestuous project of academic stress. As the academic semester spread out, I positioned myself confronting an excellent adversary, one which had grown in intensity and complexity considering the fact that my excessive school days. College guides, I fast realized, had been more disturbing, rigorous, and everyday than I had ever imagined. The workload, at times, felt like a tidal wave crashing upon me, threatening to tug me beneath.

Balancing teachers with the choice for a social life in this dynamic environment seemed like an impossible feat. The pressure to excel academically on the identical time as navigating the labyrinthine campus culture turn out to be sufficient to result in a sense of overwhelming anxiety.

Yet, it emerge as now not a battle precise to introverts; it turned into a crucible every university pupil faced. The weight of tests, the upcoming remaining dates, and the normal pursuit of educational excellence have to take a toll on each person's intellectual and emotional properly-being. However, for introverts like me, who have been frequently extra vulnerable to overthinking and self-doubt, this task may additionally want to revel in in particular daunting.

## 3OVERCOMING SOCIAL ANXIETY

Social anxiety, the elusive dragon lurking within the minds of introverted college university university college students, frequently manifests as an invisible strain that tightens its grip in social settings. Picture a university celebration as a battlefield, wherein college students collect to interact in camaraderie and amusing. For humans with social tension, even though, this seemingly danger free collecting can revel in like a treacherous terrain complete of invisible pitfalls. It's as even though an internal dragon stirs, spewing fiery self-doubt and lack of self perception, making every step throughout that social battlefield a frightening venture. The coronary heart races like a horse galloping in the direction of the precipice, sweat pours like a rainstorm in midsummer, and the mind whirls with catastrophic situations. The worry of judgment becomes a continuing specter, and the anticipation of pronouncing or doing some aspect embarrassing looms like a dark cloud. Yet, it's precisely internal this labyrinth of worry that we can embark on a courageous quest, armed with understanding and strategies to overcome the dragon of social anxiety. In the chapters that take a look at, we'll unveil the secrets to no longer virtually surviving but thriving in the realm of university social life.

As we assignment forth on this odyssey, undergo in thoughts which you are not on my own in this battle. Social tension is a not unusual foe, a silent adversary that lurks in the shadows of infinite university campuses. It prospers on isolation and self-doubt, looking for to shackle the spirits of introverted college university students. But worry not, for the adventure we're going to embark upon is honestly considered one in every of empowerment, resilience, and boom. It's a transformative day experience where you'll find out that, below the fearsome facade of social anxiety, lies the potential for profound personal exchange. You have the energy to emerge from this crucible of self-discovery no longer as a defeated warrior but as a powerful hero, armed not nice with the statistics to face the dragon however with the gadget to conquer it. So, brace your self for the adventure in advance, for it's time to confront your fears, grasp your thoughts, and unfastened up the door to a colorful and exciting college social existence that awaits past the dragon's lair.

## Recognizing Social Anxiety - Illuminating the Shadows

I such as you to recollect a normal university campus, bustling with existence, colourful with more youthful electricity. Among the students who traverse its paths, there's a tremendous company that regularly goes disregarded, now not because of the reality they choice to combination into the environment, however due to the truth they're ensnared within the shadows in their personal minds. These are the introverted souls grappling with social anxiety, the silent tormentors of their college revel in. Their stories are hidden within the back of the façade of smiles or the well-practiced art work of evading social situations. Yet, under this facade lies a international of turmoil and fear.

Once yet again, agree with this: You're about to attend a college celebration, a rite of passage for lots university college college students. Your friends are enthusiastic, the track reverberates with infectious rhythms, and the night time holds the promise of unforgettable recollections. But as you stand at the threshold of the occasion, a experience of unease starts offevolved offevolved to unfurl inner you. Your palms end up clammy, a cascade of sweat trickles down your brow, and your coronary heart gallops like a wild stallion. You can't assist however envision a big wide variety of important eyes searching your every flow, dissecting your terms and movements. The weight of judgment hangs heavy inside the air, and you surprise if you'll inadvertently end up the nighttime's leisure, a topic of mockery or ridicule. Congratulations, my friend; you've truely met social tension.

Recognizing social anxiety is much like getting into a dimly lit room and flicking at the light switch. Suddenly, the hard to understand corners of your thoughts end up seen, revealing the lurking fears and insecurities. This illumination is the first step in the route of conquering a foe that has prolonged held you captive. Understand this: social anxiety isn't always a man or woman flaw, neither is it a quirk specific to you. It is a commonplace highbrow scenario, a tapestry woven with threads of self-doubt, fear of judgment, and the relentless want for approval. Millions of human beings, from university college students to seasoned professionals, grapple with it every day.

The course to overcoming social anxiety starts offevolved with acknowledging which you're no longer on my own in this battle. It's a adventure of self-discovery and empowerment, in which you transform from a victim of your very own mind to a warrior who faces their fears head-on. But how do you recognize this diffused however ambitious adversary?

The first key lies in turning your focus inward, tuning in to the symphony of sensations and thoughts that accompany social tension. It's about becoming an observer of your very very very own psyche, a detective investigating the hidden recesses of your mind.

Begin with the bodily realm. Social tension often manifests itself through a chain of bodily signs and symptoms that can be as subtle as a whisper or as thunderous as a storm. Sweaty fingers, a racing coronary coronary heart, and an unsettled stomach are like purple flags waving in the wind, signaling the presence of hysteria. The body, in its statistics, reacts to perceived threats, making prepared you for combat or flight. These bodily responses are your frame's way of announcing, "Caution, chance ahead." Recognizing those sensations as signs and symptoms of social tension is a critical step.

Yet, social anxiety extends its grip past the physical realm. It lingers within the shadows of your mind, weaving a web of negativity and self-doubt. Imagine you're at that college party all over again. As you step into the room, your thoughts races with a flurry of thoughts. "What if I say some element silly?" "Will they pick me?" "I'm going to embarrass myself." These thoughts are like a steady drumbeat, echoing in your head, amplifying your anxiety. They are the whispers of the social tension demon, sowing seeds of self-sabotage.

To recognize social anxiety, you need to learn how to eavesdrop on those thoughts. They are the clues, the breadcrumbs that lead you to the coronary heart of the hassle. Start by means of journaling your mind at the same time as you experience stressful in social conditions. Write down the terms that race through your thoughts, regardless of how irrational they will seem. As you assessment the ones thoughts later, you'll start to see patterns emerge. You'll be conscious the routine topics of self-complaint, fear of judgment, and the selection for perfection.

Acknowledging the ones styles is just like deciphering a thriller code. It offers you the electricity to demystify the workings of your very very own thoughts. You begin to recognize that social anxiety isn't an immutable a part of your identification however a conditioned reaction, a located out behavior. Just as a expert detective unravels a thriller, you unveil the deliver of your tension, the hidden scripts that have been gambling within the historic past of your life.

This popularity, even though apparently small, is massive. It transforms the precis idea of social tension right right into a tangible adversary with extraordinary traits and vulnerabilities. It's like coming across the weaknesses of an extremely good opponent in a chess sport. Armed with this understanding, you aren't a passive victim however an energetic player inside the war towards social tension. You recognize which you have the functionality to venture these mind, to rewrite the scripts, and to redefine your courting with social interactions.

Coping Strategies for Anxiety: Unveiling Your Arsenal Against the Beast

Social anxiety, with its gnarly claws and suffocating grip, frequently seems like a persevering with beast lurking inside. It's the involved fluttering of your coronary coronary heart before a social occasion, the racing mind that hijack your mind, and the fear that others are scrutinizing your each flow into. Yet, as we delve into Chapter 3, we discover ourselves armed not with swords and shields but with a effective arsenal of coping techniques, every designed to tame this dragon of unease and uncertainty. Let's embark in this adventure collectively, revealing the secrets and techniques and strategies to no longer high-quality coping with however getting to know social anxiety.

The Art of Deep Breathing: Calming the Inner Storm*l

Let's say you're repute at the precipice of a party, your coronary heart racing, and your fingers slick with perspiration. Social tension's grip tightens as you put together to face the unknown. In this 2d of turmoil, considered certainly one of your maximum robust weapons is deep breathing. It's not handiest a smooth act of breathing in and exhaling; it's a lifeline to serenity.

When anxiety actions, it looks like a tempest raging interior, threatening to eat your senses. That's precisely at the same time as deep respiratory will become your anchor. Inhale for a depend of four, hold for 4, and exhale for 4. This rhythmic cycle will become your protect towards the hurricane. It sends a sign up your worried device: "All is nicely." With every breath, you floor yourself in the gift 2nd, breaking unfastened from the tumultuous grip of tension.

Try and study it as a magic spell, invoking tranquility in the face of chaos. As you inhale, you trap calm and readability; as you maintain, you collect energy; and as you exhale, you release tension and apprehension. The strength lies interior this simple however profound act. By mastering the artwork of deep respiration, you regain manage over your frame and mind, forging a course in the route of serenity amidst the tempest of social tension.

Harnessing the Power of Positive Visualization

Before you even set foot in that daunting social event, you possess an incredible device to your arsenal: powerful visualization. It's like having a crystal ball that foretells no longer of doom and despair but of triumph and pride. Close your eyes, my fellow traveller, and embark on a highbrow adventure in which your mind will become your most powerful first-rate buddy.

In this colorful realm of the creativeness, envision a extremely good outcome. Picture your self conducting conversations with grace, your terms flowing like a melody. See your self smiling sincerely, and experience the warm temperature of camaraderie wash over you. Imagine the room whole of tremendous faces, all eager to attach and proportion in the delight of the immediately. As you embody this intellectual panorama, you're rewriting the script of your social enjoy.

Our minds are amazing storytellers, capable of crafting narratives that form our fact. By harnessing the power of awesome visualization, you're basically penning a tale of triumph, no longer defeat. You're putting the extent for a occasion wherein tension takes a backseat, and self belief rides shotgun.

Consider this device as your non-public personal appeal, a spell you stable upon yourself to transform worry into braveness, and doubt into self-assuredness. It's the alchemical technique of turning the lead of apprehension into the gold of self-perception. In this intellectual realm, you are the hero, and the narrative is one in every of empowerment and victory.

www.ingramcontent.com/pod-product-compliance
Lightning Source LLC
Chambersburg PA
CBHW071443080526
44587CB00014B/1965